AN END TO THE
BULL

AN END TO THE
BULL

CUT THROUGH THE NOISE TO DEVELOP
A SUSTAINABLE TRADING CAREER

GARY NORDEN

WILEY

First published in 2015 by John Wiley & Sons Australia, Ltd
42 McDougall St, Milton Qld 4064

Office also in Melbourne

Typeset in 11.5/14 pt Bembo Std

© Organic Financial Group 2015

The moral rights of the author have been asserted

Author:	Norden, Gary, author.
Title:	An End to the Bull: cut through the noise to develop a sustainable trading career/Gary Norden.
ISBN:	9780730311447 (hbk.)
	9780730311478 (ebook)
Notes:	Includes index.
Subjects:	Brokers—Australia.
	Stocks.
Dewey Number:	332.62

Cover design by Wiley

Cover image (top): © iStockphoto.com/kvkirillov
Cover image (bottom): © iStockphoto.com/omergenc

Printed in Singapore by C.O.S. Printers Pte Ltd

10 9 8 7 6 5 4 3 2 1

Disclaimer
The material in this publication is of the nature of general comment only, and neither purports nor intends to be advice. Readers should not act on the basis of any matter in this publication without considering (and if appropriate, taking) professional advice with due regard to their own particular circumstances. The author and publisher expressly disclaim all and any liability to any person, whether a purchaser of this publication or not, in respect of anything and of the consequences of anything done or omitted to be done by any such person in reliance, whether whole or partial, upon the whole or any part of the contents of this publication.

CONTENTS

About the author   *vii*

Acknowledgements   *ix*

Introduction   *xi*

Part I: The need for change   **1**

1   The financial junk-food industry   3

2   Real trader psychology: our desire for short cuts 23

3   Time to break free   39

Part II: Building the foundations   **53**

4   Knowledge   57

5   Watchlists   75

6   It's a business; treat it that way   99

7   Position sizing and management   117

**Part III: The next level: incorporating more
advanced concepts**   **139**

8   Pricing in   141

9   Volatility   161

10   Become the bookmaker: how the pros trade   175

Conclusion   *185*

Appendix   *187*

Index   *191*

ABOUT THE AUTHOR

Gary Norden started his trading career at the age of just 18, trading equity derivatives for a Japanese investment house. He was the youngest ever trader in that firm's history.

Gary went on to enjoy a successful career as a trader in the City of London. At the age of 23 he became head of LIFFE options for NatWest Markets and he later held senior trading positions at Credit Lyonnais Rouse and ING Financial Markets.

Gary has also spent many years trading futures and options with his own capital, both in the trading pits of LIFFE and on computerised markets.

Since moving to Australia in 2003 Gary has developed an international reputation as a financial markets consultant, trading mentor and author.

Gary's first book, *Technical Analysis and the Active Trader*, was published in 2005 and exposes technical analysis as little more than poorly performing rules of thumb. The book was also translated into Chinese and Korean.

Gary has written for publications and websites around the world, including Your Trading Edge, Stocks and Commodities, www.trade2win.com and www.bullbearings.co.uk.

Gary has a reputation for challenging assumptions and thinking outside the box. He is driven by a love of trading and a desire to help new traders gain access to a more professional standard of information and education. Gary pulls no punches in his attacks on the parts of the financial industry that he believes lead traders down the wrong path.

2014 marks 25 years since Gary started his trading career. For more information on Gary, visit www.organicfinancialgroup.com.

ACKNOWLEDGEMENTS

To Wendy, Isaac and Anna.

It took a number of years of thinking over different formats and ideas before this version and title jumped out at me. From that moment until publication was literally just a matter of months, and credit for that must go to the team at John Wiley & Sons in Australia. Sarah Crisp was the acting acquisitions editor who helped me frame the project and was so supportive and helpful in the early stages. Following the completion of the manuscript Lucy Raymond and her team ensured that the editing, permissions and publication processes went as smoothly as possible. My sincere thanks to Alice Berry, Keira de Hoog and Allison Hiew who took me through those processes.

I would like to thank Phil Tana, Steve Hossen, Joshua Green and Grant Carter for reading through all or parts of the manuscript and providing their comments and opinions.

Finally I would like to thank my wife, Wendy, both for her support and encouragement and for reading through and editing the manuscript as it was being written.

INTRODUCTION

'Stocks are going up.'

At first reading I would suspect that most readers would not have an issue with that statement. It's quite common for us to hear such claims, and most of us would have made similar statements during our trading lives.

But what does it really mean? Does it mean that all stocks will go up? Surely not, as even during bull markets some stocks will fall. The reality of markets is that some stocks rise and some fall each and every day. Reducing this action to a simple generalisation is lazy, and poor analysis. What if the overall stock market does go up but other assets or inflation rise further? In that instance those who bought stocks may actually have lost out.

There is an incredible amount of bull$**t in this business. (I will call it 'noise' from now on.) Despite huge progress in the understanding of trader psychology and decision making, noise is still prominent in the trading and investing industry. There are a number of reasons for this (as I explain in chapter 1) but most relate back to the domination of the media by brokers and analysts, instead of traders. Currently most retail traders are, unsurprisingly, confused by all the noise and they too often end up following unreliable analysis.

In my first book, *Technical Analysis and the Active Trader*, I exposed the flaws of technical analysis, one of the most widely used forms of analysis in the business. I showed that chart patterns, moving averages and other technical tools are unreliable and result in losses for the majority of traders who use them. In this book I will expose a number of other trading myths, some of which have become accepted wisdom. Unfortunately our business is infested with myths, and trying to overturn them is no easy feat.

To me, the statement 'Stocks are going up' is akin to saying 'Cars are fast'. Some cars are and some are not—and it can also depend on what we are comparing them to. Compared to horses, cars are fast—but compared to aeroplanes, they aren't.

Would you buy a car from, or value the advice of, someone who makes statements such as 'Cars are fast'? Yet in this business, each and every day, traders are listening to and acting upon claims from such people. Here is my first piece of advice: ignore 'experts' who make generalisations such as 'stocks are going up' or 'stocks are cheap' and 'stock XYZ is going to $10'—they are unlikely to be traders; they will be sell-side individuals. Traders tend to speak differently, weighing up various risks, and the world seems a lot greyer to them (as opposed to black and white).

However, as I explain in chapter 1, most people prefer to hear simple, clear statements, whether they are valid or not. Ask a decent trader what direction stocks are heading and the answer will include an analysis of risk, a separation of different sectors or classes of shares and a discussion of various outcomes. That is why traders make lousy brokers—most retail traders and investors would think that such a response shows weakness because they have been led to believe that 'real experts' can make clear, simple forecasts. This is wrong, and is one of the many beliefs that many readers will need to unlearn.

There will be many views in this book that you may find hard to accept at first reading; at times you may even feel uncomfortable because I will challenge some of your current views and expectations. I have become used to that reaction from some sections of the trading community, particularly technical analysis–based traders. When I was presenting to a group of traders following the release of my first book I was met with the statement, 'But what you're telling us is completely different from what everyone else is saying'. My reply was blunt: 'The majority of traders lose money, so I'm quite happy to be different from them.'

In that sentence is the essence of this book. To succeed as a trader you will need to break free from the herd and be comfortable making your own decisions. There is no comfort in doing what everyone else does and failing with them. If you are someone who likes doing what others are doing, then you should reconsider trading.

As I have said on many occasions, the day that the analysis and trading techniques that I use become the norm for most retail traders is the day that I stop trading. If that sounds at odds with the fact that I have written this book, the reality is that I know it is unlikely that this book will ever become the accepted blueprint for most retail traders, as it requires too much independence of mind and resistance to accepted wisdom. In the same way that I knew that when *Technical Analysis and the Active Trader* was published, no matter how unreliable I showed technical analysis to be, it would continue to be widely used.

My aim when trading is to make good decisions based on the information at hand, and that is what I would encourage readers to learn to do. I rarely try to make predictions of future price movement. (To quote Yogi Berra, 'I never make predictions, especially about the future'.)

I would imagine this sounds odd to many readers; accepted wisdom is that traders are trying to forecast the future prices of financial contracts. However, there is a lot more to trading than that simplistic view. We need to weigh up various risks and alternative outcomes, incorporating the potential magnitude of moves as well as the probability. I will examine and explain these ideas later on.

Short cuts in trading are typically short cuts to failure. I realise that many retail traders are time-poor, with high expectations of success, but I'm not here to tell you what you want to hear — I will tell you what you *need* to hear. That will differentiate me from most writers and, as stated before, I'm comfortable with that.

Trading is a difficult business involving decision making that humans have not evolved to cope well with. Sometimes there will not even be a 'right' decision; it can depend on your risk tolerance. It is important, though, to make decisions based on sound information and to cut through the noise. I hope to show you how to do that.

Many trading courses and books teach a style of trading that involves finding an indicator that 'works' and then applying that to your chosen market. This is a simplistic way to trade. It's like a golfer only using a seven-iron; no matter how good he gets at using it, there will be times when his club can't help him. My suggestion is that we embrace as many different techniques as possible so that we can try to find the right trade for the right market condition. Market conditions change, and we need to be able to adapt our trading accordingly.

I should say that I do not claim to have 'cracked' this business or to be some kind of 'superstar' trader. I started my trading career at the age of 18 and have enjoyed more than two decades as a trader. Trading is the only career that I have known and it has been good to me, but I write this book as much as an observer as a trader. By that I refer to the many traders that I have seen fail, and the extensive research that behavioural psychologists and economists have uncovered over the past twenty years or so. This exciting research tells us a lot about our tendency to look for short cuts in our decision making, and our inability to make sound judgements. We need to learn from these studies, and I will endeavour to show what types of decisions and analysis are dangerous and ways to overcome them.

I would also encourage you to read *Fooled by Randomness* and *The Black Swan* by Nassim Nicholas Taleb. They remain, in my opinion, the best books about trading and this business in general.

This is not a 'How to trade like Gary Norden' book; the ideas and techniques I suggest are used by many professional traders, but they have not permeated through to the retail sector, due to the domination of the sell side. It is also important to state that I do not consider the ideas and techniques set out in this book to be set in stone. I am always looking for ways to improve my analysis and decision making, always looking at new behavioural research to help me understand what biases or short cuts I may be using. It is vital for all of us to constantly re-evaluate our techniques and make improvements where necessary. Don't ever think, 'That's it, I've made it!' because, as I have seen on many occasions, the market has a way of taking from those who are overconfident.

The ideas and strategies laid out in this book represent what I understand and believe to be valid at this time; if and when new ideas come to light, then I will be more than happy to revisit my ideas and make adjustments. Again, I hope that readers understand (or learn to understand) that it is not a weakness for us to state that we do not know everything and have scope for improvement. Many great thinkers, including John Maynard Keynes and George Soros, have been criticised for changing their views. However, as I will explain, changing our mind can be a strength, not a weakness — if supported by a change of facts.

I will show that it is actually crucial for traders to seek information that conflicts with their views rather than supports them — if this sounds odd now, it should become clear later. Again, this is all part of the significant difference between the ideas that I present and those you will almost certainly have read elsewhere.

At all times I will endeavour to explain why I use a certain strategy or technique so that you can understand the thinking behind it. Time-poor retail traders often want a simple trading plan or technique that they can simply deploy time and again; that is not the approach I use or teach, and if you are serious about trading you shouldn't either. To have a chance of enjoying a sustainable career you will need to understand what lies behind the technique or trade, so that you can learn from mistakes and improve your analysis and trading.

Humans are prone to short cuts when making trading decisions, and I will explain what those short cuts are and what you need to do to try and overcome them. This is one area that for some will be easier said than done.

I recognise that an increasing number of traders are favouring an automated approach and, while this book is aimed primarily at manual traders, there are still many lessons for automated traders to learn. In particular they will need to find ways to incorporate concepts such as pricing in into their trading. Each market is different and, no matter what or how we trade, our techniques will need to include an understanding of how our market works.

Finally, I must state again for the record that I do *not* believe that everyone can become a successful trader. It should be possible for many people to improve their techniques and decision making, but I doubt whether most can enjoy sustained profitability; there are simply too many psychological weaknesses to overcome.

The analogy that I use is golf. I know that, no matter how many golf lessons I have, I do not possess the ability to become a professional golfer. Even if Tiger Woods or Adam Scott were to teach me, this would probably not affect my ability to become a professional who performs in front of thousands of people. Sure, they should be able to help me improve my game and tell me the key ingredients of a good swing and getting the club into the right position, but being successful at golf is more than simply understanding what to do; it's having the ability to do that under pressure. There are many scratch golfers in the world, but how many can earn a good, sustainable living from golf? My guess is less than 1 per cent.

Daniel Kahneman, Nobel laureate and expert on behavioural psychology, is doubtful that we have the potential to control the biases that weaken our decision making. While I will show some techniques that will help you if implemented correctly, from experience I know that some people just struggle to continually make good decisions. Facing up to losses and cutting losing trades in particular is one area that many people struggle with, no matter how many times they are told to do so.

I hope that all readers will take something from this book. For those of you who have the potential to become successful traders, I hope that I can point you in the right direction and help you avoid the avoidable pitfalls that afflict so many. For those of you who may decide that trading is not for you, hopefully this book will save you from losing substantial sums to the financial junk-food industry — if that's the case, it's still a worthwhile read.

Trading is a great challenge and I wish you well on your journey. As always I welcome all feedback and endeavour to reply to all emails.

Best regards,

Gary Norden

gary@organicfinancialgroup.com

Part I
The need for change

In the first part of this book I investigate some of the problems
and pitfalls that beset traders. Some are self-inflicted, while others
are the result of poor advice and unreliable suggestions from a
sector of the financial world that I describe as the 'financial junk-
food industry'.

In order to begin our journey to a more sustainable trading
career, we first need to understand the pitfalls that we will come
across so that we can navigate through them and eventually learn to
ignore them completely.

I show that we are all prone to using short cuts, which can help
us in other areas of our life — but, unfortunately, they will hurt our
trading. I explain these short cuts and, as we progress through the
book, I continue to show ways to try to overcome them. Our focus
should be to make sound decisions based on real information.

Chapter 1
The financial junk-food industry

In this chapter...

I explain some of the reasons why retail traders can be led in the wrong direction and end up employing unreliable analysis and trading techniques. There is a strong element of mythbusting in this chapter, and no doubt I will offend some in the industry with my views. I am not easing readers in; from the outset I will be confronting you by challenging widely held assumptions and views.

Traders play a different role from brokers and analysts

During my time as a convertible bond trader I received an email from a salesperson from a large US investment bank. The email contained a research piece about a convertible bond that his firm was recommending; the piece ran to a number of pages, and it looked comprehensive. Skimming through the research I disagreed with some of the assumptions that were underlying the analyst's view that the bonds were cheap. Later that morning I received a call from the salesperson asking what I thought of the trade idea, and whether I would like to buy any of the bonds. My first question was, 'Do you have any of the bonds or will you need to go to the market to buy them?' His answer was that his firm had $10 million of the bonds on their books, ready to sell.

I now had all the information I needed to decline the trade. Here is what had probably happened: another trader sold $10 million of these bonds to this US bank, or the bank had them on its trading book. The bank then decided to sell these on because they didn't want them on their own trading book. This is usually because they believe the bonds are too expensive. An analyst was then tasked with preparing a research piece advocating the cheapness of the bonds, which required the inclusion of some dubious assumptions. The brokers could then go out and sell the bonds. This is often how the sell side works.

In my writing I use the terms 'buy side' and 'sell side'. I would expect that for many readers it's the first time they have heard of or read those terms. In the professional industry (investment banks, hedge funds and so on) they are commonly used and well-understood terms but, as with many other aspects of the professional trading business, this knowledge is not evident among retail traders. So my first task is to explain what they mean and why it's important for you to understand the difference between them. Once you do, much of the rest of this chapter, and perhaps this book in general, will be clearer.

Sell side

It is probably easier to start by looking at the sell side. The sell side of the industry is tasked with selling products such as shares and bonds. The two most common jobs on the sell side are brokers and analysts. Investment bank desks have a third position: salespeople who are in effect institutional brokers who sell to hedge funds, managed funds, and so on.

It's very important to understand that brokers and analysts are employed to sell; they construct stories, research papers and so on, designed to help them and their firm achieve their goal. As commissions and therefore income are increased by selling more, hopefully you can understand why selling is so important in the financial world. For company analysts, for example, sell recommendations are usually rare because they understand that most share market investors only trade from the long side (they buy shares), so sell recommendations will not help them achieve their goal of generating commissions for the company.

Brokers are typically paid on a commission basis; the more commission revenue they generate, the more they get paid. Personally, I see this as a conflict of interest; how can they give their clients the best advice when they need to generate commissions to earn a living? There will undoubtedly be many days each year where no decent trade ideas can be generated, and traders should be patient and do nothing. But brokers will struggle if they give that advice to their clients.

Some argue that it's not in the broker's interest to churn and burn clients, as they will continually need to get new clients. But that is exactly what occurs each and every day, hence the need for broking firms to continually advertise. If their advice was really that good, word would spread quickly and clients would recommend the broking firm to their friends. In my experience this is the exception, not the norm.

If you watch any of the 24-hour financial news channels, the various industry faces that you see and hear will almost always be brokers and analysts. They have simple, clear messages, present well and have all the attributes of salespeople — which is, after all, what they are. Similarly, quotes in newspaper or online articles are usually from brokers and analysts too; they are the faces of their organisations, and presentation is as important as knowledge for many of them. Sell side individuals who appear regularly on TV or in the wider media can command higher salaries simply due to their profile, regardless of their performance or the accuracy of their recommendations. (If sell side individuals were paid on performance, like traders, I'm sure they would on average earn far less than they do.)

Buy side

Traders, hedge fund managers and even pension (superannuation) fund managers are on the buy side of the business. These are the individuals and teams who make the trading and investing decisions, and they carry the risk of the trades. They receive daily calls and emails from those on the sell side trying to sell them various trades or investments, but their job is to critically analyse those recommendations, as ultimately it is the trader or fund manager's job to make the trading decision. Those on the buy side rarely appear in the media, and it does not matter how they present, because they are paid to deliver in terms of trading profit or fund performance. Those on the buy side must weigh up the risks of each trade; they stand to lose their job if they consistently enter into losing trades. Compare that with your broker; if he or she recommends a dozen trades to you, which you enter into, and they all lose, which is most likely?

a) The broker loses their job.
b) You lose your trading capital.

Bearing in mind that the broker has been successful in achieving good commissions for his or her firm, I would suggest the most likely answer is 'b'.

My role as a trader is obviously very different from that of brokers. I need to be able to see through the sales techniques and come to my own view on whether these are good trades. Conversely, when I want to sell one of my positions, I instruct our sales team to pitch the trade to their clients. Clearly I will only be exiting a trade if I believe there is little profit left in it, but there are always other opinions and it's up to the sales team to find reasons to place the position elsewhere. You can see why good salespeople are crucial to trading desks if they can help traders get in and out of trades.

As a trader, there will be days when I decide there is nothing to do. As I am not commission-driven, I am more than happy to sit with my current trade or sit out of the market if that is what my analysis tells me is the right thing to do. My only goal is to keep making good decisions, as good decisions will lead to a long-term, sustainable trading career.

So it should be evident that traders are very different from brokers and analysts. Traders need to be good decision makers, and they need to be patient. They have to weigh up various risks and outcomes, which means that trading decisions are not always simple and clear cut. Sell side individuals, though, are involved in creating reasons and stories why traders should enter into a trade.

If I were to go back to a car analogy, I would explain the roles this way. Analysts are like mechanics — they understand the theory of how the car should run, but that doesn't mean they can drive the car around a racetrack in the best or fastest way; theory and reality can differ. Brokers are like car salespeople — they are not experts on how the car works (although they know enough to sell to customers) and they also usually don't possess the ability to be a racing driver and get the car around the track intact and quickly. They are very good at selling cars, though.

Traders are the racing drivers of the industry. They should understand the theory that analysts (mechanics) do, but they must then apply it to the real world. They must understand the past, but they need to make decisions on how they see the road ahead. Regardless of whether the track has been clear on previous occasions, racing drivers are not racing the previous lap; they are racing the current one, and this time might be different. They cannot predict what will happen in three or four laps' time, because there are too many uncertainties beyond our control. What our driver (trader) can do, though, is to constantly re-evaluate the situation and make adjustments when necessary. Traders do not need, and rarely possess, sales skills, and so would tend to make lousy salespeople.

Don't get me wrong, brokers do have a place in our industry, in the same way that we use real estate agents and car salespeople. A broker's role should be to assist a trader, if required, in executing a trade and advising on order flow; brokers that are good at this are well worth using. It is vital, though, that traders learn their analysis and trading techniques from other traders, not from brokers and analysts. As I will discuss, in many instances this does not happen.

The 'other' junk-food industry

Some years ago, when my son was about four years old, he asked me, 'Why do junk-food restaurants sell food that is [allegedly] bad for you?' (He didn't use the word 'allegedly', but for the benefit of any lawyers who are reading this, I have added it!) The answer was, of course, simple: 'Because people want it' and, as we all know, successful businesses are usually built on giving people what they want. Sometimes though, as with junk food, what we want is not good for us.

In trading we have our own 'junk food' industry: an industry that has evolved to give people what they want, because that is how firms make money. Unfortunately, though, what retail traders typically want is not what's good for them. As Cass Sunstein and Richard Thaler state in their book *Nudge*, firms have more incentive to cater to irrational practices than to eradicate them.

Let's examine a typical new retail trader. What does he want (and what doesn't he want) to hear? The first thing he wants to know is that he can and will be profitable. He wants to believe that a simple trading plan with some easy-to-understand entry and exit points can lead to a profitable trading career. He wants a form of analysis that does not take up much time, but that somehow can still deliver great results.

The newbie typically does not want to spend a significant amount of time learning about the mechanics and fundamentals of markets — they want a form of analysis that cuts through that hard work. They do not want to hear that trading is hard work and that many will fail. With these ideas in mind, the new trader will seek out those who provide the messages he wants to hear.

Luckily (or not) for most new traders, the industry is more than happy to tell them what they want to hear. And so begins the exchange of funds from the new trader to the industry. This is all a part of the financial junk-food industry.

One of the key reasons why retail traders are so attracted to the financial junk-food industry is because of the skills of the sell side individuals who dominate it. Their job, as we have discovered, is to bring new entrants into the markets and then to sell them as many contracts or products as they can. A large percentage of the books, courses and presentations for new traders are actually written by analysts and brokers. As many retails traders don't know the difference between traders and brokers, they will use these resources when learning to trade.

Take this example from an advertisement for a seminar for would-be traders. The presenter of the seminar who was supposed to be teaching the new traders was described as '... formerly head of technical analysis ... for over 17 years. Learn from an experienced trader'.

Not only is this person an analyst, but he is a technical analyst (which is often just an astrologer of the markets, as discussed later). He is not a trader—the statement saying so is incorrect.

As both Taleb and Kahneman have explained, people prefer simple, clear messages and the sell side is very good at providing that. They tell you that there are straightforward paths to trading success, or 'secrets' that they are only too happy to share (for a price).

I'm sorry to burst the bubble, but there are no secrets and there are no easy ways to success—but there are many short cuts to failure. If anyone had a simple technique or strategy that could be easily copied and implemented, then they would not be sharing it with you. To navigate through the noise you will have to avoid the tendency to veer towards the simplistic, and take on board ideas that may seem more complex and even less certain. As Taleb has argued, people tend to favour and reward the providers of misleading information, who are typically optimistic and overconfident, rather than reward the usually more sobering truth-tellers. As you progress through this book, I would ask you to keep that thought in mind.

Accepted wisdom — trying to separate fact from fiction

As I suggest in the introduction, there are many pieces of accepted wisdom, generally spread by the sell side, that I believe do not stand up to scrutiny and are not accepted by most professional traders. Accepting these 'facts' and incorporating them into their trading is another contributing factor to the failure rate of retail traders. So let's look at some of these.

Myth one: Longer term trading is easier than short-term trading

The first one that I will discuss is the view that short-term trading is too volatile, and that trading over a longer time horizon is easier. The first point to make is that, if longer term forecasting is easier, why do analysts have such a poor record with their recommendations? Studies have typically shown that analysts' forecasts are inaccurate — and often by a wide margin. Studies have also shown that most long-term fund managers under-perform their benchmarks.

Almost all the professional futures traders that I have met (including those wily old floor-traders) trade with a very short-term outlook (intra-day). You may be surprised to learn that most investment bank traders are also short-term traders, trading in and out of the order flow that their institution sees. (By 'order flow' I mean the daily activity [orders] that comes to the bank's desk, often as a result of sell side actions.) There are actually very few longer term proprietary traders at investment banks — too many have suffered large losses. So while the bank's sell-siders are pushing long-term views, the bank's own traders and capital are put to use in short-term strategies typically benefitting from the business that the sell-siders generate.

If we look at this issue from a trader's perspective (as opposed to the perspective of an investor who may be looking for gains including dividends and tax incentives) I would argue that short-term trading offers a better outlook.

If we were to examine any contract (it could be AAPL.US stock or gold futures) and I were to ask you to tell me where it will be trading in say six months' or 12 months' time, you would probably find it very difficult to give me an answer that you have any confidence in. Of course, analysts (both fundamental and technical) have their targets and opinions but, as I have already stated, these are usually incorrect. If we take the view (which we should) that the essence of trading is to gain a good understanding of our risk and reward so that we can implement good trades, how can we do so on this long-term horizon when we really have little idea where the contract might be trading such a long time away? So many events could happen over a 12- or even six-month horizon that I simply do not believe that traders can make robust judgements.

However, if I were to ask you to give me your estimate of where AAPL.US stock or gold futures will trade tomorrow, it is likely that you would be able to provide a possible trading range that turns out to be more reliable. What if I asked you to tell me where those contracts will be in one hour's time? Or even in two minutes' time? Your estimates of potential highs and lows and a trading range, and therefore risks and rewards, will improve the shorter the time frame we look at.

Also, the potential for event risk diminishes with a shorter time frame. We cannot even imagine the range of potential events that could hit markets over a six- or 12-month period: EU debt issues, China slowdown, US debt ceiling, US Fed tapering — these are just some of the issues that have occurred over the six to 12 months just past, and the reality is that we have no idea what could happen over the coming year or so. Option contracts, and in fact all insurance contracts, have embedded in them the fact that there is more event risk, more risk possibility, over the longer term compared to the short term. Yet many traders simply ignore this fact when it comes to other products such as equities.

Since behavioural finance studies have shown that traders and investors often make poor (some would say irrational) decisions, I have seen it argued that trading for a short-term horizon must be more difficult. The argument is that this irrationality is only a short-term phenomenon and that over time rationality will win. I simply do not hold this view.

My view is that because the poor decision making of many participants is constant and ongoing, so too is the noise associated with them — it will not decrease over time. In fact, I believe that it is easier to understand the issues that participants are weighing up today than it is trying to understand what might affect their decisions in the next week, or month or year.

Some readers will point to the charts that all brokers use that appear to show that stocks have always gone up over the long run. Surely these prove that in the long run it is easier to judge the stock market, because it always goes up. Well, I don't disagree that over the very long term many global share markets do rise (there are some, including Japan, where this has not been the case)—but this does not mean that individual stocks all rise. The indices that are charted regularly kick out weak stocks and replace them with stronger ones; in that way, they are almost rigged to show stocks going higher.

Knowing that stocks always rally over the long term will not help investors in Eastman Kodak, Enron or WorldCom. We need to understand, too, that those bullish charts usually include reinvested dividends, which most participants don't pursue. Clearly, though, other markets, for example commodities and currencies, do not only go one way over a long period of time. They can have trends, usually due to fundamental reasons, that last for a few years, but they are not viewed as markets that will always rise over the very long term in the way that equities are viewed by many.

While it is clear to me (and I hope now to you too) that there is less risk, and the prospect for better decisions, with shorter term trades, this view, as you will likely know, is completely at odds with accepted wisdom. Accepted wisdom is that the short term is full of volatility and noise, and over the longer term all this smooths out. As we proceed further through the book you will see that my belief in short-term trading is central to the techniques that I advocate. Let me also state that, of the hundreds of professional and bank traders that I have worked with, the vast majority opts for short-term trades.

Myth two: Closing prices hold the key

The next piece of accepted wisdom that we will dissect is the view that closing prices are the most important ones to follow. A large number of trading systems, courses and techniques use entry and exit points based on a contract's closing price. I have heard many, mainly technical analysis supporters, claim that the markets are opened by amateurs and closed by the professionals, and I have certainly encountered this view among retail traders.

I have traded many products over the years, in most cases as a market-maker. (Market-makers are the wholesalers of a market, setting prices and providing liquidity, usually for large institutions.) The markets that I have traded have been diverse and include FTSE options, Japanese convertible bonds and German interest rate options. I can categorically state that in each and every market that I have traded, the bulk of the business is received and dealt with in the early part of the day. In fact many of the big trades and decisions are made before the market even opens.

If we think about this from the perspective of a hedge fund or investment bank traders (the larger players), it makes sense to trade as early as possible. These traders arrive for work at least an hour before their market opens and they spend this time analysing what has happened overnight and deciding what they want to do today. This could be to exit a trade, to add to an existing position or to enter a new trade. Let's say the trader decides that he wants to enter a new long position (he wants to buy); clearly he will do this because he thinks the market of that contract will rise. Why then will he wait until the close to enter the trade? If he thinks that the market will rise he will want to buy as soon as he can. That is why market-makers often have to make prices before the market opens (especially in over-the-counter products)—institutional traders demand a price prior to the market opening because they want to get the trade done before the market starts its daily move.

So the bulk of the decent new business takes place prior to or just after the market opening. However, these are rarely market-on-open orders (orders to be executed at the market opening, whatever price that may be); they are usually limit orders (orders that have a defined price or limit). What then typically happens is that the market-maker will endeavour to get out of the position as quickly as possible, hopefully for a profit. There are also a number of Volume-Weighted Average Price (VWAP) orders, more commonly used by pension funds, managed funds, and so on. In order for the broker to execute these well, they also need to execute a significant portion of the order on the open. This is where there is lots of volume, and so by definition any volume-weighted price that is given prior to the market opening must be traded to a reasonable degree on the open.

There are other orders that come into markets during the day, but unless there is some new information (a subject we will look at later) there is usually not the same volume of new orders as we see on the open. Towards the close, activity can often become quite erratic. In my experience there are two predominant forces at work.

Firstly, traders who have been unable to execute a limit order at the price they originally wanted might have to 'go to the market' to fill it. So these are traders who have essentially got the market wrong on this day, and now need to pay above what they wanted (or sell cheaper than they wished). If the market has been rising (and they missed out on buying earlier), then these traders will push it even higher into the close, and vice versa on a down day. A trader who got the market right and bought early, before the rally, won't need to trade into the close.

The second type of trader that we often see towards the close is the one who wants to try and move (some would say manipulate) the closing price to try and help their existing position, or simply to make the contract look stronger or weaker than it really is. There can be many reasons why bank traders in particular do this. One of the first lessons that I learned as a young trader of Japanese equity warrants was that other traders were moving share prices around at the close to help them execute their business for the next session. Learning this was crucial to my trading and led me to ignore the closing price itself and examine the circumstances around the price. For example, if a stock moved higher in the last thirty minutes or so on thin volume and with nothing else happening to similar stocks, I would be very wary of the closing price; someone may be looking to sell and hoping that enough traders use the high closing price as a reference. Whether we like it or not, this type of activity takes place, which is why it is so important to understand the context of any graph or data we are studying—the price alone and even the price and volume is usually not enough.

So market closes can be times of erratic behaviour, and in my experience many professional traders prefer not to trade during this period. We would generally only trade on the close if we had to—either a sign of a bad day, or trying to move a closing price to a particular level. The idea that the activity around the close and closing prices themselves are where the best business occurs is just not borne out in my experience across a range of markets. I have discussed this topic with traders in markets that I haven't traded, and they have reported similar activity.

So I would strongly disagree that closing prices are of greater significance, and I certainly would not be basing a trading system or entry and exits around a closing price. In my opinion the use of closing prices by technical analysis traders is more likely because it provides simple set-ups, rather than being due to important price action.

Myth three: Technical analysis is reliable and successful

Possibly the biggest myth for traders to overcome is that technical analysis is reliable. If a new trader was to look for trading education anywhere in the world, it is almost certain that they will end up buying some kind of chart- or indicator-based course. I will not dwell too long on this issue because I discuss it at length in *Technical Analysis and the Active Trader*. The methods that are used by technical analysis supporters to attract new followers are, in my opinion, just a part of the financial junk-food industry. The claims of technical analysis supporters, both on the reliability of their tools and the underlying philosophy behind them, just don't stack up to serious scrutiny.

For the purposes of this book I will briefly examine why so many retail traders are enticed into using technical analysis. Firstly, it is due to the sheer abundance of technical analysis courses and books. If we look at one of the key reasons behind this, we come back to the junk-food argument. Retail traders want analysis and trading tools that are simple to learn and can be easily replicated time after time, with easy-to-understand entry and exit points. The junk-food principle leads to the industry providing what traders want, and technical analysis tools are perfect for the job.

The concept of trading with the trend, doing what everyone else is doing, also fits well with what most retail traders want to do. They seem to take comfort in doing what everyone else is doing, even if ultimately most others fail. You may ask, 'How can traders fail if they are trading with the trend?' The answer is that technical tools are very poor at spotting the early days of trends, where the real profits are; they tend to get traders in later in the trend, and typically fail to spot the end. Trading with the trend is something that is easier said than done for many who try it. I once worked with a trader who had been a very successful option trader, but wanted to try his hand at futures trading. His favourite saying was 'the trend is your friend', and that was his guiding strategy. He did well for some months but lost everything one afternoon. Watching someone you know lose everything they have worked for, in just a few hours, is not a pleasant experience—I did try to persuade him to cut the trade much earlier, but to no avail—but it is something that I have learned from.

Leading on from the discussion about technical analysis is a more general examination of how you choose the trading style or technique that you will trade with. Here we find another problem that afflicts retail traders, namely that they tend to choose a style that appeals to them. For example, those who believe in astrology will seek out the astrological-based strategies, such as Gann theory, phases of the moon, star signs, and so on. I have to say that I hadn't even heard of Gann during my 14 years in the City of London and was amazed, after having spent time with retail traders, how popular this theory and other astrological-type styles are among retail traders. Similarly, those with a more mathematical or engineering background will seek out more mathematical-type strategies; they look at markets as a problem that can be solved in the same way a maths question can be solved.

The problem with what these people are doing (and this is common) is that they are choosing a trading style based on their beliefs rather than on how markets actually work. It is vital that we trade the markets rather than trade our beliefs, and to do that requires a completely different approach, one that I'll expand on later.

We know from behavioural finance studies that we are all prone to biases and heuristics. The word 'heuristic' is well defined in *Thinking Fast and Slow* by Daniel Kahneman as 'a simple procedure that helps find adequate, though imperfect, answers to difficult questions'. There is no doubt that many heuristics are used by traders to cope with the difficult questions that trading poses. While I will explain some of these later on, an example would be the way that some people see patterns and correlations where they don't exist. It has been shown that people can see patterns in random events; because we find randomness hard to deal with, we come up with explanations (patterns in this case) for what we see.

So knowing that we are all prone to heuristics, it is important to understand them and to work out ways to mitigate their influence on our trading and decision making. (As Kahneman states, it is unlikely we can eliminate them completely.) Looking for a trading style that suits your personal beliefs is very likely to be an expression of one of your heuristics. We need to form objective views of what is happening in the markets, and then find the right trade for the situation. Central to this is the fact that we cannot simply adopt the same trade or technique time and again, because the market situation is likely to be different on different occasions. The problem here for those who use technical analysis is that the markets always look the same when you are looking at markets in the same way. Their short cut of patterns or indicators prevents them from seeing the whole picture. I will show ways of overcoming this problem.

Myth four: Scan through as many contracts as possible to increase your chances to find a trade

This myth typically goes hand in hand with technical analysis–type techniques — for example, using chart patterns or indicators. The theory is that we are supposed to learn an indicator that we are told is reliable and then we scan through as many contracts as possible looking for the particular indicator. We are told that scanning through more contracts gives us a better chance of finding a good trade. Putting aside the issue of whether these indicators really are reliable, I strongly disagree with the idea of scanning through lots of different contracts, because you are likely to end up trading something you know little about. The idea that all markets are the same and therefore any indicator applies equally to any market is simply not true. Also, chart- and data-based trading excludes any form of context, and often context is vital to understanding what is really happening in a market.

When you trade a contract that you know little about, you greatly increase the risk and that can be a recipe for substantial losses. Some of the biggest losses that I have seen or heard about, even at investment banks, have stemmed from traders entering positions on contracts or products where their knowledge was less than it should have been.

My suggestion is to specialise; study and trade one contract or sector (for equities) and trade it well. Over time we may wish to expand the number of contracts we trade, but only when we have a firm idea of the first. There is an edge to be had in specialisation in an industry where many people try and trade anything and everything. Most successful businesspeople are specialists in their field; they do not believe that by branching out into new industries they will increase opportunities. Far from it; they are more likely to be increasing risk. Most investment bank traders are also specialists; there will be a dollar–yen trader and a separate euro–dollar trader on an FX desk, for example. They each need to learn and understand how participants in their market work, and being a specialist gives them an edge.

A story from my time at NatWest some years ago demonstrates this theory in action. A very experienced and successful trader of UK government bonds (Gilts) was asked to join the small team of proprietary traders at the bank; these were the few traders who were allowed to trade almost anything they wanted. So, from being a specialist in one product, this trader was now allowed to trade whatever he wanted. I caught up with him a couple of months into his new role and he told me that he was finding the new position far more difficult than his previous one. He explained that as a Gilt trader he knew that market well and he could quickly establish the risk and rewards of each trade he examined. Now he was a 'prop' trader, he had brokers ringing up with trade ideas in a wide range of products. On the face of it, there were opportunities everywhere, but his experience led him to believe there could not possibly be so many good opportunities. He found scanning through different markets and contracts far more difficult to assess good trades than being a specialist in one, and his profitability was affected too. He made more money as a specialist Gilt trader and soon he asked to return to that desk. John Mauldin once wrote that we know less than we think we do and, while this is true in general, it is even more valid when we scan through many different contracts.

Myth five: Fundamentals, company and economic data are not important

As noted already, a common theme among the myths that are so widely embraced by retail traders is that they supposedly make life much simpler. Analysis, knowledge or techniques that might be considered more challenging are typically replaced by others that are more likely to appeal to traders who, at the end of the day, are basically regarded by the industry as an easily replaced source of revenue.

I am sure that all traders and readers are aware that daily, weekly and monthly, companies, governments, central banks, agencies and so on publish data and information. Some of this is economic data such as GDP and retail sales, relating to countries. Other data, such as earnings announcements, capital raisings and so on, are announced by companies. The financial junk-food industry understands that the average retail trader is unlikely to understand, or want to understand, economics and company balance sheets, and so on, and so it has come up with a myth—you don't need to understand all of that. Both technical analysis supporters and even many of those who follow a more fundamental approach simply tell you that because others are analysing this data, you do not have to; it's all in the price. The fundamental analysis–based firms will advise you simply to follow their analysts' views, which is understandable but will make you reliant on them—which, of course, is what they want.

The concept that 'everything is in the price' is far more complex than is taught and practised. If so many traders and investors do not analyse all the data and simply refer to what they believe others to be doing, how can everything be in the price? Surely the price must also reflect all those who have little knowledge or understanding of all this information. As a retail trader, how do you know if you are following the real experts or all the noise traders? Furthermore, in trading, as with many businesses, the edge is usually in being early on a trade. If you wait for others and then jump in, you may well be late on the trade; you will be the one that the early comers will be selling to.

Returning to the racing driver analogy, while racing drivers do not need the level of understanding of engines, gearboxes and suspension that the mechanics and engineers have, they still need to have a decent knowledge of them. I can't imagine Sebastian Vettel returning to his pit crew and telling them, 'Something isn't right, but I haven't a clue what it is'. Or, worse, a racing driver who guesses what might be wrong and leads his crew on a wild goose chase. Good racing drivers understand which part of the car isn't working so that they know what needs fixing. During a race, when they perhaps can't get the problem fixed, understanding what is wrong helps them to make the correct adjustments. Our job as traders is similar to a racing driver during a race. I do not expect readers to build up the sort of in-depth knowledge that analysts have, but we do need to understand these data because they affect our trades. As with any knowledge, it really comes down to how you implement it—analysts have a lot of knowledge, but usually apply it poorly. Traders (and racing drivers) may have less in-depth knowledge, but our edge must come from the implementation of that knowledge.

You should know by now that I am not trying to simplify the business (although cutting out noise will reduce a lot of the fluff). I must state that I believe it is important for all traders to have an understanding of the economic data and company announcements. At the very least it will help our decision making around what is being priced in and how we need to position ourselves, which I will discuss later on. I find it hard to understand how retail traders think they can have a long-term, sustainable trading career without this type of knowledge. The financial junk-food industry telling you that you don't require this knowledge is just them telling you what you want to hear—they need to do that to maintain a viable business.

Myth six: Traders need to buy on the offer side and sell to the bid side of the bid/ask spread

When you buy and sell a contact, what price do you trade on? It is commonly assumed that we must buy from the offer side and sell to the bid side of a bid/ask spread.

For example if we are trading MSFT.US stock at a current bid/ask spread of $37.40 to $37.45, then to instigate a buy trade we would buy at $37.45 and we would sell at $37.40. Most have been told that we must buy on the offer price and sell to the bid, and some platforms—notably some CFD and FX platforms—only allow traders to trade in this way.

It might seem that we are only talking about a few cents for shares or a few pips for FX trades, but for active traders these small amounts will add up to a considerable sum over the course of a year. The reason some companies' platforms only allow customers to buy from the offer and sell to the bid is because it is the spread where the firm makes its money. Investment bank traders, pit traders and all market-makers have long known that the bid/ask spread can itself provide a good source of profits. As I will demonstrate in the last part of this book, there can be significant profit from taking the small amounts of money that others deem to be insignificant. Every successful trader that I have known has not only understood the value of the spread, they have actively used it to their advantage. This provides them with further edge over those they trade against.

If you want to make a living from trading or simply want to trade in a more professional manner you need to understand the impact that the spread can have on your trading, and you will need to start trading as the real professionals do: by placing buy orders on the bid side and sell orders on the offer side of the spread (for instance, in the earlier example we try to buy at $37.40 and sell at $37.45). Of course you need to weigh up the current conditions, and if the contract is moving rapidly in one direction you may have no choice but to trade on the 'wrong' side (amateur side) of the spread, but such occasions are the exception, not the norm.

Think of it this way: those who set the bid/offer spread (that is, those who buy on the bid side and sell on the offer side) are effectively paying the wholesale price, while those who trade against them are paying retail rates. To increase our profitability we need to pay wholesale prices, for there is obviously less edge for short-term traders who pay retail prices.

Summary

- Understand the difference between 'buy side' and 'sell side' individuals, and ensure you learn your trading techniques from the right people.
- Avoid the temptation to head down easy street—the financial junk-food industry will be waiting for you. You may want simple ideas and solutions (don't we all), but in this business they are likely to be short cuts to failure.
- Technical analysis and many of the assumptions that underpin it are simply not as reliable as supporters claim.
- Specialists have edge.
- Knowledge of economic data will be required.
- Use the bid/ask spread to your advantage.

Chapter 2

Real trader psychology: our desire for short cuts

In this chapter...

I show some techniques that I believe help to overcome some biases and heuristics. I outline some of the heuristics that have been uncovered so that you can learn more about our flaws and weaknesses. We need to understand these and try to overcome them if we are to build a sustainable trading career.

If you were to ask the average financial junk-food commentator about the psychology that drives market participants, you will usually hear the words 'greed and fear'; markets, we are told, are driven by greed and fear. While this is true to a degree, maybe more at market extremes, there is a lot more to the psychology of traders and investors than simply greed and fear.

In recent times the field of behavioural finance has exploded with a range of research and knowledge of how we make decisions, and all traders need to understand these concepts. In particular, a range of biases and heuristics have been shown to affect (or afflict) decision makers. It is therefore vital that we learn more about them and try to find ways to overcome as many as possible.

Daniel Kahneman, Nobel laureate and one of the leading figures in behavioural psychology, is pessimistic as to whether we have the ability to control our heuristics. I must say that in general I tend to agree; however, in the next section of the book I will show how to overcome some of them.

Whether or not most people can consistently employ these techniques is another matter, in the same way that, no matter how many times I tell a trader to cut losses quickly, whether or not he does so is ultimately a test of his own discipline.

Representativeness

Representativeness is a widely used heuristic whereby we estimate the likelihood of something happening by how closely it resembles something we have seen in the past. As a result, we can place too much emphasis on a small amount of evidence that we believe represents something more than it really does.

Robert Shiller, Nobel laureate, sums up the representative bias succinctly:

> ... people tend to make judgements in uncertain situations by looking for familiar patterns and assuming that future patterns will resemble past ones, often without sufficient consideration of the reasons for the pattern or the probability of the pattern repeating itself.

I hope that by now you will be able to easily identify a type of analysis that Shiller's statement sums up perfectly, namely technical analysis.

In fact, another well-documented aspect of representativeness is that it can actually lead people to see patterns and reasons behind truly random events. People assume that events or information that look the same must be correlated, but the reality is that this is not necessarily the case. However, we can struggle to come to terms with the concept of randomness, and so looking for patterns is a tactic that we employ. We will come back to randomness later in the book because it is an important topic to examine.

Of course, as with any of the biases, employing representativeness doesn't always mean that we will lose money. Trading is essentially a fifty–fifty business, so it's hard to get it wrong all the time, no matter how poor the analysis we use. Those who employ this bias will be subject to random rewards and therefore may keep using their analysis methods. However, while we use the representative bias to make our decision making easier, it obviously does not make for better decision making—so we need to try and overcome the temptation to use it. Once again, ditching the use of chart patterns and many other technical analysis tools will greatly help in this regard.

Another aspect of representativeness is the tendency for people to 'predict' unlikely events, stemming from a failure to understand probability. What would your answer be to the following question, again courtesy of Amos Tversky and Kahneman?

> Linda is 31 years old, single, outspoken and very bright. She majored in philosophy. As a student, she was deeply concerned with issues of discrimination and social justice and also participated in anti-nuclear demonstrations.
>
> Which alternative is more probable?
> a) Linda is a bank teller.
> b) Linda is a bank teller and is active in the feminist movement.

If you are like the vast majority of people who have read this question then you will have answered 'b', Linda is a bank teller and is active in the feminist movement. However, this cannot be the more probable alternative; being a bank teller and active in the feminist movement is a subset of being a bank teller, so being a bank teller must be more likely. This is an example of us receiving a small piece of information and making a less probable judgement. As with all the biases and heuristics, it does not matter how intelligent you are, we are all prone to them. When the 'Linda' question was posed to undergraduates at a number of major universities in the US, roughly 85 to 90 per cent also chose option 'b'.

Quite often we hear or read forecasts from sell side individuals along the lines of 'Stock XYZ will rally 30 per cent in the next six months'. This can be particularly true of technical analysts whose use of various anchors, including past lows, Fibonacci levels and so on, can lead to numerous calls of such magnitude. These sorts of forecasts are similarly an aspect of representativeness in that they ignore probability. It is the exception rather than the rule for contracts to move, say, 30 per cent in a few months — yet many sell side individuals make such calls quite often. As Kahneman states, 'Extreme predictions and a willingness to predict rare events from weak evidence are both manifestations of System 1.' System 1 is our more instinctive decision making system and can often use short cuts and make mistakes. For more difficult decisions we need to employ System 2, which requires a lot more thought. I discuss these concepts in more depth later in this chapter.

Availability bias

Availability bias is closely linked to representativeness. It is when we estimate the frequency or probability of an event based on the ease with which we can remember it. As with representativeness, we often use only a small amount of 'information' to make such judgements. If I were to ask you whether it is more likely to have a stroke or be diagnosed with lung cancer, many will think about the number of instances they personally have known of each and base their decision on this. Obviously, though, (unless we are a doctor or nurse) we will only be aware of a small number of each; any answer we make based on this information will be unreliable. Note, though, that because there are only two options we still have a 50 per cent chance of being correct, and if we were right we would probably attribute the success to our wisdom. (This is the self-attribution bias, where we attribute success to ourselves, whereas failure is someone else's fault.)

Let's take a retail FX trader who trades a few times a month. His last trade was to buy AUD at 0.915 and he loses money on the trade. He may well say to himself that he won't buy at that price again; it is not a good price to buy. But the reality is that the currency has traded hundreds of thousands of times and his trade was of little consequence. He is basing his decision on a small amount of 'information' using the availability bias. Importantly, there is no thought of context in his decision; what else might have been occurring in the markets when he last traded? Context is a vital ingredient in all our trading decisions and must be incorporated into our analysis.

Anchoring

The concept of anchoring has been around for some time but it was propelled further into mainstream psychological thinking by the work of Tversky and Kahneman. When faced with making a decision where we are unsure of the answer, we can look for and use any (even useless) 'information' (noise) that we might come across, even if it's unrelated. The noise that we use is referred to as an 'anchor', as we anchor our decision to it.

In one of Tversky and Kahneman's most famous studies they constructed a spinning wheel that was numbered from one to 100. First the wheel would be spun and then participants were asked general knowledge questions such as 'What percentage of UN nations is African?' The wheel was rigged to stop at either 10 or 65 and was spun before each question. If you're thinking there was no way that the spinning of the wheel would influence the answers given, then you are wrong. From a range of questions, the median response when the wheel stopped at 10 was 25, while when the wheel stopped at 65 the median answer was 45. When faced with questions where they didn't know the answer, people grasped at any 'information' that was handy. Similar studies have been conducted and they confirm the existence of anchoring.

Anchoring has been identified as a significant heuristic among traders, investors and analysts, and it can also be difficult to overcome. For many participants it can be unclear what information is good and what might be useless, but I will address this topic in the next section. I would also suggest that using current prices as a basis for making decisions on longer term targets constitutes a form of anchoring. (I've already raised the issue of the difficulty of long-term forecasting, but it is also relevant in this context. Does today's share price, or the price of any contract, really have any relation to where it will be in six or 12 months' time? I doubt it, but most of us will use today's price as a starting point. Again, I can see today's price having relevance tomorrow, but it is less clear that it is the case for a year later.)

I also believe that many technical analysis tools are in fact forms of anchoring. Support and resistance levels incorporating previous highs and lows, and so on, are not reliable forms of analysis; they are using unreliable anchors. An interesting aside here is that we saw with the spinning wheel study that participants did not use the exact number from the wheel; they knew that would be seen as silly, so they modified their answer slightly. This is exactly what technical analysis supporters do with orders based around support, resistance and other anchoring-type levels; they advise you not to use the exact price level, as that would make your trades too obvious. They believe that by using a level a few points away they are being smarter and the market will never know that you have been using an easily seen level. The reality of course is that such a strategy is not smart, and savvy traders are well aware that many orders are placed slightly away from the actual technical level. So dumping the use of technical analysis will also help to diminish the use of irrelevant anchors.

Conservativeness

Conservativeness is the tendency for people to cling to an opinion. Once they have formed a view they are slow to change their opinion, which can lead to an under-reaction to new information. We have been led to believe that people who change their mind or change their decision are somehow weak. Politicians who do this are likely to be classed as 'flip-floppers' and having made a 'U-turn', both of which have negative connotations. However, this negative view can be incorrect; in fact, if the situation has changed since the first view was formed, then it is correct to change our mind. As Keynes (who was a great trader in addition to his more famous work as an economist) was famously quoted, 'When the facts change so do I'. Conservativeness can also be caused by overconfidence.

Overconfidence and overoptimism

If a teacher asks their class, 'Who is in the top 50 per cent?', far more than 50 per cent will put up their hand. It may well help students get through the year if they think they are better than they are, but a better frame of mind to take is to work towards being in the top half of the class. Being overoptimistic about our chances can help us get through life, but for traders realism is the frame of mind we should embrace.

People can be overconfident and overoptimistic for a number of reasons. The self-attribution bias, where we can attribute success to ourselves but blame others for losses, will lead us to have more faith in our decisions than is warranted. Many are also prone to the illusion of control, where they think they are more in control than they really are; this in turn leads to overoptimism.

For example, in an experiment by psychologist Ellen Langer, one group was given a $1.00 lottery ticket while the second group got to choose their $1.00 ticket. When asked how much they would sell their ticket for, the first group would sell for $1.96 while the second wanted $8.67; those who selected their ticket wanted more for it, because they believed they had more control over the outcome. This is clearly absurd.

If you have been told that most traders make money, or that a certain trading technique works time after time, you too are likely to be overoptimistic about your chances of success. Hopefully I have already provided a dose of reality to help overcome this, but if not there is more to come!

Hindsight bias

Hindsight bias can also lead to overconfidence in that, after the fact, we believe that we knew the outcome. Most people I know say that they knew that internet stocks were a bubble by 2000—but I suspect if I examined the trading and investing records of those people, I would struggle to find evidence. If we look through any past data it can be easy to think that we can spot the trends, but in real time the markets are never so simple. One key aspect of trying to overcome hindsight bias is again to understand context and also try to place yourself at the time of the events.

If you look at markets through the rear-view mirror using charts and past data, you significantly increase the risk of hindsight bias.

Without knowledge of context and an honest ability to judge what someone at the time would have thought, any use of past data is doomed to suffer from hindsight bias. It is an understanding of context that can help us to overcome this. As Kahneman, Taleb and others state, we believe that what looks clear today was predictable yesterday, and this illusion that we understand the past makes us overconfident in our ability to predict the future.

Confirmation bias

Confirmation bias is also linked to overconfidence. It's a heuristic that is widely used by traders, and one that I believe is possible to eliminate, or at least mitigate. Confirmation bias is the tendency for people to find information that agrees with their view, while ignoring contradictory evidence. It is used every day in various ways; for example, those with conservative political tendencies will watch and read like-minded news media such as Fox TV in the US, the *Daily Mail* or *The Daily Telegraph* newspapers in the UK and *The Australian* newspaper here in Australia. Those on the progressive side of politics may read *The New York Times* in the US, *The Guardian* in the UK or *The Age* here in Australia. They are constantly seeking views that confirm their own, and so will not be able to find reasons why they might be wrong (many probably don't want to). Even when contradictory evidence appears, those who are prone to confirmation bias will tend to underweight or ignore it completely. Meanwhile, any evidence or data that confirms their original view is accepted. Confirmation bias (as with hindsight bias) can lead to the illusion of validity, where people believe that their views are more valid than they really are.

While looking through an internet trading forum (for research purposes only) I came across someone who claimed to have developed a system that had worked on Australian stocks over a certain period. One of the self-proclaimed 'gurus' of that site then went away, tested the system over that same period and enthusiastically reported back to eager would-be users that indeed the system did work. This is nonsense. The only way the system could be properly tested would be to use a completely different time period, preferably in real time. A bunch of eager and overconfident traders would undoubtedly have then paid for the system, and would almost certainly have been disappointed with the results.

If we go back to Keynes's quote, 'If the facts change so do I', this statement suggests that Keynes was looking for and willing to take on board new information. To succeed as a trader it is vital that we implement strategies to overcome confirmation bias. As scientists know, you can only test the strength of a hypothesis by seeking to disprove it; we must adopt the same approach in trading.

Cognitive dissonance

The final weakness that we will investigate (sadly there are many more, but for the purposes of this book we need to move on soon) is how we cope with evidence that our beliefs are wrong. We have seen already that many people can be slow to face up to new evidence and/or are reluctant to seek such evidence, but the reality is that, whether we seek evidence or not, if at some point we are wrong we will need to face up to that. You may not be surprised to learn that we do not like facing up to being wrong—in fact, it can cause considerable mental conflict, termed 'cognitive dissonance'.

Cognitive dissonance is a term used in psychology for the discomfort or stress that we feel as a result of holding conflicting views. For example, if a trader buys a stock because he thinks it will rally and it actually falls, he will suffer the anguish of believing his trade should have made money (while actually suffering a loss).

Our dislike of facing up to our poor decisions, and the resulting cognitive dissonance, leads us to incorporate further poor decision making procedures into our analysis. We saw earlier that some people simply ignore or underweight contradictory evidence (confirmation bias). Certainly a well-documented issue is the 'status quo bias', where there is a strong urge to do nothing. For many people it seems that keeping the status quo is the default option and a way of trying to overcome the distress of their previous actions; again, compare this to Keynes's quote about changing his mind when the facts change.

It is well known that too many traders and investors struggle to cope with losses. Prospect Theory shows that we gamble with losses (because we are trying to avoid them), but that we prefer to bank safe gains; this idea was expanded upon by Hersh Shefrin and Meir Statman. Their studies showed that people did everything they could to avoid a loss, due to the mental anguish it would cause, so they would hold on to losing stocks for far too long. On the other side, exiting a profitable trade leads to happy feelings, so people would sell winners. They called this phenomenon the 'Disposition Effect', arguing that people were predisposed to holding losers and selling winners — which obviously will result in poor outcomes.

I can't remember how many times I have heard traders and investors say something like 'It's not a loss until I sell' or 'The market will always come back' after a trade or investment goes badly wrong. Here we have examples of loss-aversion and status quo bias caused by the distress of facing up to a bad decision or bad outcome.

Trading will result in losses in the same way that playing football will result in bruises (or a series of broken bones, in my case); we have to accept this. If you struggle to face up to losses quickly, then they can get out of control. In the next section I will explain the disciplines that I believe are required in the next section, but this is one area where knowing what to do is one thing—the difficulty comes with whether we can implement the right course of action with consistency. I do not believe this can be taught and can't say whether most people can overcome the issues associated with losses. I can say that I have seen traders improve, particularly if there is a way to learn from the loss (and also if we can keep the losses small). If I want to win during my trading career, then I will know that exiting losing trades quickly is imperative. As soon as we run a losing trade we are effectively relying on hope — this must be avoided, and if we are determined to make good decisions then cutting losing trades quickly and avoiding the reliance on hope should be incorporated into our trading.

It is important to state that facing up to losses is not inconsistent with playing to win — it's actually a key part of playing to win. If we run losses then our chances of winning diminish. In the same way, poker players know that they can't win every hand but it's vital they don't lose too much money when they are losing.

Top golfers know that if they're in trouble on a hole it can be better to take an over-par bogey than to try and play a miracle shot to get par with the potential consequence of dropping more shots. Decisions and course management such as this can play a vital part in who ultimately wins the golf tournament; so even for golfers, handling a bad shot or decision is crucial.

I will discuss position management later, but for now I will suggest a simple strategy that I have employed since my very early days as a trader: if I hold only winning trades, I can only make money. I learned this while trading during the crash of the Japanese stock markets by watching other traders, and initially myself, hold losing positions that we thought would come back to profit. I realised relatively quickly that this usually did not happen and so I always cut losing trades when they were showing only a small loss. My trading book became significantly easier to trade as a result.

Trading is unlike anything else we do in terms of the sheer number of decisions that we have to make. We rarely make other decisions that have financial impact; for example, we might buy a car or move house every few years. But trading requires decisions every day, and the volume of decisions means that we will also be faced with bad decisions more regularly than we are used to. This is why it is imperative that we have an ability to handle losses, and are able to deal with them quickly. If you run a losing position then you will face that agony every day you have the position. If you cut it, then it's gone and you can move forward.

I have heard it argued, 'But what happens if I cut the trade and then it does well? I'll feel really annoyed'. First, what happens if you don't cut and it gets even worse? Second, cutting a losing trade does not mean we can't re-enter it. It is possible that we were early on the trade, but if we get stopped out at a small loss we can get back in if conditions suggest so and still make money. Quite simply, though, holding losing trades is gambling—and we are not here to gamble.

A broker demonstrates biases in action

A simple real-life example will show some of these biases in action. Early in 2013 a broker/advisor (sell side person) recommended three stocks to his investor base. By the end of November, over six months later and with the stock market having rallied, two of his stocks had fallen by over 10 per cent, a clearly significant under-performance to the Index. The third stock had rallied slightly more than the market.

So in November 2013 I asked him what he had done with the two stocks that were down over 10 per cent. I understood that he was a longer term investor rather than a trader, but just because we take a longer term view does not mean that we should accept large losses. Also, the various biases apply to us all, traders and investors alike. He answered that they were both good companies, he only buys good companies and he was happy with the positions. There was no element of 'I might be wrong' in his thinking. He did not place stop loss levels and he completely disagreed with my tight stop losses because, he claimed, market volatility could take him out of the position. This is essentially an 'I am right and the market is wrong' belief. Running losing positions is like gambling with losses, but is common due to the heuristics that we have discussed.

The issue is more interesting because one of the stocks that had fallen had issued a profit warning only a week or two before, stating that margins were under pressure and the outlook was difficult. As I am sure you are aware, it is the exception for firms to report bad news, and they prefer to be upbeat and positive for obvious reasons. So here we had a company stating that trading conditions were difficult and the market did what it should; it revalued the stock downward. But the broker was clinging to his initial view, formed several months prior, that it was a good company and a good stock to own. (Five months after he reaffirmed his liking for the poorly performing stocks, the stock that had received a profit warning announced another earnings warning and was down by around 30 per cent. The broker's unwillingness to embrace new information, and stubbornness to avoid taking a loss, is costing his clients even more.)

This is conservativeness in action; there has been new information but the broker has ignored it. Leading into this is also the status quo bias: doing nothing is the default option, while the cognitive dissonance of facing up to a bad trade also makes keeping the position the easiest course of action. The typical statements from investors whose decisions have gone wrong, namely 'I am in it for the long term' and 'It isn't a loss until I sell' are classic status quo bias views.

Remember, 'when the facts change so do I'—the facts had clearly changed, but the broker held on. Confirmation bias was also at work, in that the bad news was ignored in favour of whatever good 'information' (noise) confirmed the broker's view. He was relying on hope; the stock may go up, but it will likely take some time, and in the meantime the money that was used to fund that investment would have been better even in the bank. There is an opportunity cost to holding losing trades, particularly over several months like that one. I'm also sure that we can all see that overconfidence was a key factor there too.

Even if, at some point in the future, the stock does rise, it will not be as a result of that broker's original analysis being correct. The company's situation will have changed since his original decision, even if his analysis hasn't. If it does rise in the future it must be as a result of something new occurring. Of course, it is unlikely that the broker will realise or admit to this; self-attribution bias will lead him to believe that he was right all along.

I must also add that it is possible that the first decision to buy this stock was a good one at the time, but things clearly changed. As I discuss later, we can only assess a trade at the time of putting it on, and if the situation changes so must we.

This type of example occurs each and every day, and I am sure every one of us has faced it. I hope that by explaining the biases that are influencing our decisions I can help to show you what needs to be done to make better decisions. Hopefully you now understand the psychological flaws and forces that are leading you to make poor decisions at key times.

I also want to bring in another of Keynes's beliefs: namely that markets are like a beauty contest where we are trying to forecast the beauty that everyone else will vote for. This is a very interesting and valid statement. We can only profit from a trade if others also form the same view—because we do not move the market. That is why our approach to trading must include an understanding of how other market participants think and operate. If the broker in my example likes the stock but no-one else does, he will lose money—and, given the new information at hand, it should have been clear that the market was going to sell this stock.

The other trait that I believe is a significant failing of many traders and investors is a lack of humility. The broker stated clearly, 'This is a good company, the share price will rise'. I get very concerned when I hear such statements. Whenever we enter a trade we must acknowledge the possibility that we are wrong. In fact, this is one of the most important things that we must face up to, as I explain in the next section. There is a world of difference between taking a contrarian view and saying 'I am right and the market is wrong'. Humility and general good practice means that we should always have a stop loss to protect us on the occasions when we are wrong.

More on System 1 and System 2

Finally for this chapter, I want to bring in an idea of Daniel Kahneman's from his excellent book *Thinking Fast and Slow*: the concept that we have two thought processes, System 1 and System 2. System 1 operates automatically and quickly, with little or no effort and so can be at the mercy of our heuristics. System 1 makes easy and lazy decisions that can be wrong, but it is hard (or almost impossible) to switch it off. Kahneman coined a wonderful phrase for System 1: WYSIATI (what you see is all there is), and this encapsulates some of the points that I have made, particularly about technical analysis. People are happy to use the small amount of 'information' in front of them and ignore other possibilities.

System 2 allocates greater attention to tasks and takes up more mental effort. If I asked you to multiply 35 by 18 you would need to use System 2. For the purposes of our trading we need to engage System 2 as much as possible, which requires us to slow down, take in as much information as possible and weigh up possibilities that may not have previously occurred to us. According to Kahneman, the expert on heuristics, overcoming biases takes considerable effort. System 1 can't do this; we need to slow down and use System 2.

Summary

- We are prone to a number of biases and heuristics, which are unreliable short cuts.
- Trying to eliminate or overcome these is vital if we are to succeed.
- We need to face up to losses and cut them quickly.
- We need to employ System 2 to help us overcome poor decision making.

Chapter 3

Time to break free

In this chapter ...

I look at the mindset that we need to adopt if we are to take on the difficult job of being a trader. We've already learned that much of the accepted wisdom among retail traders is unlikely to be useful, and we've investigated our psychological weaknesses. Now we need to start the process of looking at alternatives and improvements. Before we investigate the analysis and decision making techniques that we will need to employ, we must first be in the right frame of mind.

Why do you want to trade?

It might sound like an odd question, but undoubtedly a lot of people take up trading for the wrong reasons. If you have been enticed into trading by an ad in the media claiming that trading can offer a simple way to make a fortune, then hopefully after reading chapter 1 you will now understand that this is less likely than the ad stated. Even if you are successful, it will not be easy. We must avoid the trap that the financial junk-food industry is setting in an effort to separate us from our hard-earned money.

There are times, particularly during equity bull markets (because they are widely reported in the media), when stories abound of everyday folk making huge sums in the markets. This will then attract new traders who want to make this 'easy' money and don't want to miss out on the riches that markets can supposedly offer. For many people there is nothing worse than watching their friends or neighbours make more money, whether it's sustainable or not. Once again, during these times, take a long hard look at the situation and understand that easy bull markets will always end — typically with a fair degree of carnage for the average retail trader. No matter what the market conditions are, one fact has remained constant for generations: most traders lose money. Keep that fact in your mind when considering a career as a trader.

It is imperative that you enter the business with realistic goals and an understanding that trading will require a good deal of knowledge and some difficult decision making. The idea that someone can sustain a successful trading career over the long term by spending just 20 minutes or so a day on analysis, as claimed by many, is simply untrue for the vast majority who try.

Many of us like to stretch ourselves mentally; we like challenges and are driven by a desire to test our decision making skills against the toughest conditions. If you see yourself as that kind of person, then that at least is a better headspace to start from. I see my job as a trader as weighing up some difficult choices and trying to make good decisions. If I can consistently do that, then profitability and longevity should result. Notice here a subtle difference in emphasis: my focus is not simply on making money; it's on making good decisions. If I focus on money, I may end up taking too much risk or making bad choices. If, however, I focus on trying to make good decisions, then profits should result. But, importantly, there will be times when I reduce risk because I see that as the right thing to do. My decisions are not always based on what will make me money; other reasons include 'what will save my capital' and 'what is the right thing to do'.

This attitude really comes into its own during those bull market occasions (for equity traders) such as the internet bubble of the late 2000s. While most traders were chasing the potential large rewards, but taking risks in doing so, most of the experienced and better traders that I know ignored many of these trades. For a while they made less money than some of the retail risk-takers, but ultimately most of the risk-takers got burned while the better traders continued on.

For those who are successful, trading can offer great rewards, both financially and in terms of fulfilment; consistently overcoming the challenges that trading brings provides a great feeling of achievement. But this success does not usually come easily and you should be prepared to work at it, understanding that none of us starts off being the best trader we can be and that we're always learning and trying to improve.

Lifestyle implications

In this section I will assume that the new trader has spent a considerable period of time (at least three to six months) trading a demonstration account before deciding to switch to real money. We're looking at the choices that she faces now; there are still some potential psychological hurdles to overcome.

The decision on whether to trade is more difficult for someone who has financial commitments than for a young person living at home with her parents. This is not an insignificant issue to deal with. If you have commitments such as a home loan or private school fees, then before you even start trading each month you effectively have to make this amount just to break even in terms of your personal finances. The problem here is that this situation can appear to many traders to be like starting each month with a loss, and the loss needs to be overcome. As Kahneman and Tversky show with their studies and subsequent Prospect Theory, people are far more likely to take risks when they are facing a loss. To illustrate this point, let's look at two of Kahneman and Tverksy's problems:

- Problem 1: Which do you choose? Receive $900 for sure OR a 90 per cent chance to get $1000.
- Problem 2: Which do you choose? Lose $900 for sure OR 90 per cent chance to lose $1000.

The probabilities in all examples are the same, but if you're like most people you will prefer the sure $900 profit in Problem 1 but would choose the gamble in Problem 2. This highlights one of Kahneman and Tverksy's most important findings: we behave differently when faced with profits and losses. I would say that many experienced traders would wholeheartedly agree with this idea and would even wonder why it's controversial. However, in the world of economics it has always been assumed that decision makers behave rationally and there's no distinction between gains and losses.

So, returning to the new trader with large existing financial commitments, there is great potential for viewing the start of each month as being in a loss position before you even start. If we compare this to a young person living at home, with few financial commitments, then the latter is likely to be in a clearer frame of mind. Consider a situation when markets are quiet and we are struggling to find any trades. Sometimes the best thing to do is nothing—but if you need to pay thousands of dollars of bills that month, doing nothing is easier said than done. You can see how traders can be led to make trades that might be marginal or poor in an effort to try and generate profits. The ramifications can be many and significant; not only the potential for losses, but also psychological damage from losing on a trade that you might not have executed in different circumstances.

We understand this problem; we now have to find a solution. You may be relieved to know that it does not involve divorcing your partner and selling your house (after all, that can be even more expensive). First, you must remain in your current job; while it's not ideal to juggle a job and embark on a trading career, this is necessary to begin with. This way you know that your bills are paid and you can start trading with a clear mindset. If possible, during this time put some funds aside into a savings account. These funds are in addition to your trading capital and are being built up to provide reserves, a form of comfort. Do not even think about leaving your job until or unless you have at least six to 12 months of consistently successful trading, with few if any significant drawdowns. If it's always your intention for trading to be a secondary part of your life, then you will obviously not consider leaving your permanent career; but bear in mind that, over the long term, it's very difficult to juggle the two roles. I know very few people who trade properly and carry out another job, in the same way that it's hard to be a successful golfer while still working 9 to 5.

By the time you transition from your previous role to full-time trading you should be comfortable that you can be successful, and also that you have ample reserves of capital just as a safety net. If in doubt, take the conservative option and delay trading for a living. You are not missing out by delaying; you are making it more likely that when you do start you'll be in the right frame of mind.

You need to be an independent thinker

This should be no surprise after reading chapter 1. In order to sustain a long-term trading career, you will need to have the ability to think and act independently. We must remember that most traders lose money, so being different from the majority is a badge we should wear with pride.

If you want to trade like someone else, if you like to blame others when something goes wrong, if you seek others' views before you make a decision, then in my opinion you don't have the characteristics of a trader. Simply trying to follow the trend without regard for context or weighing up other possible risks is also a way of relinquishing responsibility and exhibits that trait of 'it's okay if I fail if everyone else fails'. Good traders may sometimes go with the trend or sometimes against the trend; they will trade whichever way they believe offers the best expected return or provides the best trading opportunity. Good traders don't simplify a contract's performance by trying to categorise its trend without investigating context, alternative outcomes and a range of possible future outcomes.

One of the best pieces of advice I've ever been given was told to me by a veteran options trader from the US, who remains the best trader I have ever worked with or seen in action. I was about 22 at the time and don't mind admitting that it took me some time to fully appreciate and use his advice. He told me, 'You will make the most money when you have the opposite trade to everyone else.' He wasn't saying that we should always trade against the herd, rather that we should at least be prepared to do this, as these trades can offer us the best reward. By definition, being able to profit from these situations requires the ability and strength to trade independently, to make our own assessment of a situation and, if required, to trade against the trend or the prevailing view.

As technical analysis is the study of trends and how to get on them, it is highly unlikely, both in my view and experience, that technical analysis users will be able to implement the concept of having the opposite trade to the crowd. The whole point to following the trend is that the market is ahead and knows where it is heading. Obviously I disagree with this last statement.

The trading position that causes me most concern is to be long equities (a long position is when you have bought) when most others appear to be as well. Of course there are times when my analysis tells me to do this, but nonetheless, being long equities with everyone else always keeps me on guard. Equity participants are known for their overtly bullish nature; only a very small percentage ever trade from the short side. And many of the larger participants, namely pension funds and the like, are typically mandated to buy shares no matter what the market situation. This means that equity prices can often reflect too much exuberance, hence my concern when I have long equity trades in bullish markets — which I imagine sounds odd to most readers.

But coming back to the advice that I was given and subsequently have seen in action, if you are wrong when many others are wrong too, the losses will be significant and it can be extremely difficult to exit the trade. The more experience I have gained in this business, the more comfortable I've become holding contrarian trades; I think that many experienced traders feel the same.

So my suggestion is that being a trader requires the ability and even the determination to be an independent thinker. We should embrace trading as being a challenge of our ability to analyse situations and make decisions, and we're trying to find out if we are good at it. Don't rely on tips from someone at the pub, or from a friend; don't rely on advice from a sell side person (without first analysing the trade for yourself); don't go asking around internet forums for the views of others (I still don't know how we can be sure that the self-proclaimed experts on the forums really are experts); make your own decisions and then find out whether or not you have the temperament and ability to be successful.

By making our own decisions we can blame no-one else, and this is how it should be for traders. So often I have heard retail traders blame their broker or analyst or someone else for a loss. Profits always seem to be their doing, but losses belong to someone else. You may remember from chapter 2 that this is the self-attribution bias and, among other things, it inhibits our ability to learn from our mistakes because we simply attribute them to someone else. We need to stop this practice, and we do so by taking responsibility for everything we do. The reality is that many people are uncomfortable taking such responsibility, in which case they should not trade.

Ditch technical analysis

My criticism of technical analysis is well known by now, but for the sake of completeness I need to discuss this briefly. There is nothing advanced or complex about technical analysis, and it will not improve your decision making. Many technical analysis tools and beliefs are nothing more than expressions of the representative bias that I have explained, and representativeness is a bias that we need to avoid. The case against technical analysis is substantial and is laid out in *Technical Analysis and the Active Trader*, but for this book I will make the following point: in the 14 years that I spent on trading floors and in trading rooms in the City of London with hundreds of professional traders, I knew none who used technical analysis actively. When we were formulating trading ideas on the desks that I worked on, we never discussed chart patterns, support and resistance levels or trendlines. The only people that I witnessed referring to technical analysis were brokers and technical analysts — the sell side.

Of course I look at graphs, but not to get trade ideas or to make deductions about entry points or patterns. When I look at a graph I am trying to deduce how its participants are positioned. I will look at whether the contract has been rising or falling, but not just to jump on the trend—rather, to help me see what others have been doing in order to help me weigh up possible outcomes.

A common theme through this book is the need for us to ignore noise and instead concentrate our time on more robust information. Ditching the unreliable claims and beliefs of technical analysis is another step down the road towards eliminating noise from our trading.

Trade to win

For the first 14 years of my trading career I only traded among professional traders on trading floors and in trading rooms. It can be a dog-eat-dog world characterised by a hunger among all traders to win, to make money. Some traders will do almost anything to win (that's a whole different topic) but a common characteristic of all of the best traders that I have known is that they hate losing.

After moving away from the City of London and during the research for my first book I encountered the world of the retail trader for the first time. This is the world of short cuts and technical analysis—but also, for the first time, I encountered traders who were not always trading to win. This might seem odd, but I heard statements such as 'I'll put $10 000 into a trading account and I'm prepared to lose that' or 'I'll only trade with what I am prepared to lose'. If you go into any business prepared to lose a certain amount of money, then indeed you will lose. Not only are you prepared to do so, but you will be competing with people who are only playing to win.

The capital that we place into our trading account is the capital that we need to trade with; it is not what we are prepared to lose. In fact, quite the opposite: we need this capital to trade with, so why would we be prepared to lose it? Of course we must not trade with money we don't have, or with funds that will affect our lives if lost, but this is different to saying, 'I am prepared to lose $X'. This latter view is a negative philosophy that suggests a half-hearted approach. If you take the view that you are prepared to lose a certain amount then that view will influence your trading, whether you're aware of it or not.

If it turns out that your trading does not go well, you could decide to stop before the funds have been used up; in fact this would be the right thing to do. This is different from saying that you are prepared to lose a certain amount. Here we have tried trading, found out that we are not good at it, and then decided to stop because if we can't do it successfully then we won't do it at all.

I can illustrate the problems with the 'I'm prepared to lose $X' attitude by recalling an evening at the Crown Casino in Melbourne a few years ago. I like to play poker, which I view as a very difficult challenge. The variety that I play, Texas hold 'em, like other forms of the game, requires an understanding of mathematics, but also psychology — in particular, trying to weigh up what other players might be thinking.

It was my first visit to the Crown's world famous poker room (it's a great venue) and I was only playing on a low-stakes table, maximum starting balance of $200. I started playing around 11 am on a Friday and played throughout the day. It was a very tough environment to make money, especially for a new player such as myself. By around 10 pm I was in profit, but only a small amount — perhaps $50. Then things started to change; from around 10 pm onwards on this Friday night the table started to attract players who were having a good night out with their friends, part of which was playing some poker. Chatting to them in between hands I heard the following type of statement again and again, 'I've come with X amount of money and I am prepared to lose that, I'm having a good time'.

The next three hours were extremely profitable for me and a couple of other players on the table, at the expense of these good-time players. I made a few hundred dollars and only left the table at 1 am because I was too tired. The good-time players who were prepared to lose almost always did so — they lost everything they came with. Watching them play I saw that they would make risky and sometimes irrational decisions. It was clear that those who were playing to win had an advantage over those who were prepared to lose. I'm not saying we won every hand, as sometimes risk can lead to reward, but over the few hours there was a steady flow of money from the good-timers to those who had a more determined mindset.

This was the first time I had seen this 'prepared to lose' mindset in action and, while I was happy to have come away with a good profit, I was equally staggered that people could adopt this attitude when dealing with their money; I couldn't understand how people could be happy to lose money in a competitive environment.

As well as offering the opportunity for profits and losses, poker and trading have another thing in common: they are both often viewed as being 'cool' or exciting pastimes or occupations. This is another reason why people attempt to take part in them—needless to say, it's not a valid reason.

Successful traders do not gain enjoyment simply from taking part in the business—they will only enjoy the business if they win. This does not mean that we chase any profits—we must of course stick to making good decisions, and profits will come from that. However, our dislike of losing will mean that a succession of losses will see us re-examine whether to continue. We don't have to lose all of our trading capital before re-evaluating, and we don't get excited or take enjoyment from participation.

If you gain some kind of a thrill from entering trades, then this is cause for concern. This type of behaviour more closely resembles addiction (such as compulsive gambling) than it does the behaviour of a successful, professional trader. One of the reasons I like day trading, where we make dozens of trades a day, is that it desensitises us from the trades. Trading is less likely to produce excitement when you make dozens or hundreds of trades a week—it becomes a normal procedure, in the same way that a four-foot putt for par doesn't cause as much nervousness or excitement for a professional golfer as it does for me, because the professionals complete thousands a year.

So our mindset must be that we are playing to win, and this will be done by consistently making good decisions. We are not prepared to lose our trading capital; in fact, quite the opposite: our trading capital is the means to our livelihood, so why would we be prepared to lose it? Loss-making trades are inevitable, but we must try and learn from them so that we can improve. In an industry where so many professionals are playing hard to win, anyone who does not do so is likely to be providing profits to the pros. The best traders that I have met are competitive by nature—they want to win at everything they do, and they hate losing.

Random rewards—a dangerous business

It has become common in recent times for traders to adopt the technique of backtesting a contract and then implementing a strategy that the trader believes has a high probability of success over the medium to long term. Such a technique is based on a few underlying assumptions: first, that the backtested, historical data is relevant to the future; second, that any short-term losses need to be overlooked and the strategy continued because it will generate profits over the long term; third, such mechanical, pre-determined techniques eliminate the possibility for our weak human psyche to negatively affect our trading. As with much of the accepted wisdom that abounds in this business, I can see why this technique has been widely accepted—however, you will not be surprised to learn that I disagree with this approach.

The first assumption, that backtesting through historical data will uncover a successful strategy, is deeply flawed. The past is just that, and actions and trades that occurred over the preceding period are actually unlikely to be repeated in the future. You cannot and will not be able to analyse future risks and rewards simply by analysing what has occurred in the past.

Let's take a stock that has been trending gently higher for the past six months, with no significant declines over that period. Does the fact that it has not suffered any large declines for six months mean that it cannot fall sharply in the future? Of course not. Those who have backtested a strategy over this time period, though, will not be weighing up anything other than what has occurred in the past when they work out the risks, rewards and profitability of their chosen indicator or tool. This is the reality for this type of analysis and trading, and it is nowhere near as robust as its users believe. Those who use this approach will often be hit with unforeseen events, because anything that has not previously occurred is deemed not able to occur. Of course none of us can foresee every potential event, but it's important that our analysis allows us to weigh up outcomes that have not yet occurred. This is a step that I will explain later and is a major omission for most traders.

I will tackle the second two assumptions together because they both relate to our psychology. The procedure of simply employing a certain strategy, technique or indicator again and again because we think it's profitable over the long term can actually be very dangerous for us. First, both successful and unsuccessful trades will look the same to us, which I believe is unhelpful. We might enter a trade that loses money, exit and then simply do it all over again hoping it will be profitable next time. I can't see how we can learn from this. Second, this technique introduces us to a very dangerous situation: namely the problems associated with random rewards. We do the same trade again and again and sometimes we make money and sometimes we don't: our profits (and losses) are therefore random. Research on both animals and humans has shown that being rewarded randomly carries huge dangers.

In the past, tests have been carried out on birds or monkeys, with two groups of animals: one fed randomly, the others fed after performing a certain task (for example, ringing a bell). The group who was being fed randomly introduced certain rituals that the animals thought resulted in being fed. Birds might spin around or perform an elaborate dance in the (false) belief that what they were doing was influencing the food supply.

Some time later the feeding stopped, and researchers wanted to learn how quickly both groups would stop whatever activity they had thought had resulted in food arriving. The group that had to perform the specific task stopped doing it quickly when the food no longer appeared. They had learned cause and effect and, as soon as the food didn't come, for example after ringing the bell, these birds no longer wasted their energy ringing the bell.

Those who were fed randomly, however, were not aware that their efforts (dancing, and so on) were not the cause of the food—and so, even after the food stopped appearing, they continued to perform the ritual even until they starved to death.

I believe this is a significant danger with the technique of simply employing the same strategy time and again in the belief that over the long run it will be profitable. Rewards become random, and random rewards are addictive and hard to change. For example, what would you do if your strategy had eight losing trades in a row? This is like the dilemma that faces lottery players who are thinking of changing their numbers. They always ask themselves, 'What happens if I change and then my old numbers win? I'll be really angry!'

Far from being easier psychologically, this approach actually causes many problems. After eight losses, if you still believe in your system, you just need to keep going; surely you must be due some winners. Personally, I would hate to keep going with the same tactic even though it has failed for so long. I would see myself as a kind of trading version of General Haig in WWI—just keep sending them over the top; hopefully we have enough troops to get through.

So while the mechanical way of trading may tackle one aspect of human psychological frailty by taking the decision making away from the trader and into the hands of the system, it introduces another, probably more dangerous, one. It becomes very hard to improve your decision making and trading. The usual course for traders once they have finally decided to ditch a system after a string of losses is to look for another system, and so the process starts again.

Remember that the underlying assumption (that we can work out the future probabilities and profitability of a strategy by finding out how it performed in the past) is wrong. All we can find out is how it performed in the past, and this will only be applicable to the future if the future is the same as the past—an outcome that is highly unlikely. As I explain in *Technical Analysis and the Active Trader*, numerous robust studies have proven that indicators that have performed well in backtesting fared poorly when employed in real time—that is, the coming future period.

My opinion is that I would rather try to overcome the issues of discipline than be drawn into a situation where I am receiving random rewards and losses for doing the same thing over and again. I need to have some understanding of context behind my trades and outcomes, otherwise I can't learn and improve.

If a certain type of trade or decision has even a small run of losses, I will want to change as quickly as possible. As someone who is playing to win, it just doesn't seem right to keep going and hope the next trades win; hope isn't your friend in this business. Also, if we aim for a higher success rate of trades, our rewards will cease to be random; they will be the norm.

Again, contrary to the current prevailing view, I do aim for a high percentage of winners and believe that if I were only hitting a 50 to 55 per cent success rate then my analysis is little or no better than flipping a coin. We might then employ any trading philosophy and simply rely on money management, as the technique itself is of little use.

Summary

- You must have realistic ambitions and be prepared to work hard.
- Don't be afraid to think independently.
- Play to win.
- Don't rely on random rewards—they are addictive.

Part II
Building the foundations

In part I we examined where traders can go wrong. In an essentially fifty-fifty business, it is widely acknowledged that over 80 per cent of traders lose money—so, clearly, most are doing something badly wrong. Conversely, there can be good profits for the minority who do well. I should add here that, of the minority of successful traders, some will achieve success through chasing risk or simply through luck (please refer to *Fooled by Randomness* by Nassim Nicholas Taleb for more on this). For most of us, though, relying on luck and risk-taking will result in failure, so I hope that by now you will want to focus on trying to make good decisions.

In part II we begin the process of building our trading and analysis techniques. We do this with some key concepts that must be incorporated into our methods:

1 We must preserve our capital.
2 We need to be able to trade in as many market conditions
  as possible.

3 We need to understand the context of the price action we are seeing.

4 We need to employ our System 2—more thoughtful decision making that tries to overcome unreliable biases and heuristics.

Preservation of our trading capital is crucial and should be our first goal. We can only take advantage of good trading opportunities if we have funds to trade with. During the course of my career I have seen too many traders lose their capital chasing great profits, when in fact they were taking too much risk. I am actually a very conservative trader, hence I place preservation of capital even ahead of making profits, as doing this helps to prevent me from chasing risk. Another golden rule that I use is if in doubt, do nothing; stay on the side and observe how the trade would have fared. This way I can learn without necessarily having to lose money doing so.

To enjoy a sustainable trading career that lasts for years and decades will require the ability to trade in as many market conditions as possible. Too many retail traders can make money in trending or bullish markets but struggle in bearish stock markets or when volatility picks up. We need to gather the knowledge that will enable us to trade in the more difficult times without taking on too much risk. Doing so will provide us with opportunities that others don't have.

Context is another important topic. Retail traders and technical traders often try to eliminate context from their analysis because it's complex to weigh up. But I would strongly argue that eliminating context is a short cut that will produce poor analysis. It is not, for example, sufficient to say that, since a stock fell sharply from a price of $5.50, it's likely to do so again. If the stock fell after a profit warning, then it was the news that sent the stock lower, not the price. No matter what price it was trading at that time, it would likely have fallen (if the news wasn't priced in). It will therefore be wrong to simply believe that if the stock rallied back to $5.50 at some point in the future, that this level will be a resistance point. Not only was the price of $5.50 not the reason for the previous fall, but today's market conditions will be very different from before; we need to trade today's market, not last month's, or a previous set of circumstances.

Another example that I use to demonstrate the importance of context is the 2002 Winter Olympic speed skating race that was won by Australian Steven Bradbury. Bradbury was trailing in last place for most of the race before the leaders collided and fell, leaving him to skate past and claim gold. Now let's say the race is to be rerun on the same track, with the same competitors. We ask two bookmakers to make up the odds for the race: one watched the race, and the other has simply seen the result. They will likely produce two different sets of prices, but the one who is most likely to make the best prices is the one who watched the race. It is very unlikely that all the leaders will fall again, and so Bradbury would be unlikely to win the same race again. An understanding of the context of the result is therefore crucial.

With trading we need to monitor the market conditions and develop an understanding of the context of the current price action. It's not enough for us to just look at one price or to quickly refer to a graph and expect to understand what is going on.

Gathering more (good) information will help to slow down our decision making, enabling us to make more informed decisions. There are other short cuts, too, that we must overcome, and I'll show ways to do so.

Bank and hedge-fund traders are supported by a number of different personnel, such as product controllers (who judge liquidity) and risk managers, who assess various aspects of their trades. Also, senior traders, heads of trading and so on, offer an oversight role. This means that there are a number of checks and balances in place. Not only does this help in areas such as risk assessment but, as Kahneman states, such processes can also help by slowing down the decision making, thereby enforcing the use of System 2–type analysis. Private traders, however, don't have this support crew; they alone must therefore act as risk managers and product controllers, so they have a greater need to slow down the process.

The chapters in this section outline the foundations to achieving these four goals and I refer back to these four core points throughout. There are no secrets in this section; indeed, the suggestions I make are incorporated by most of the good professional traders that I have worked with. It's just that, for reasons discussed previously, they haven't made it to the retail trading world. If there is one overriding theme that flows through this section it would be knowledge. We should learn as much as we can (about the right things) and we should keep learning.

The knowledge and information that we must gather will doubtless be much greater than most retail traders use, and I make no apology for the extra effort required. Not only do I consider knowledge a core ingredient for sustainable trading success, but also gathering and using a variety of information can help overcome some of the short cuts that people are prone to. We are actively trying to engage our System 2 by slowing down the decision making process. I will also explain the difference between information and noise, as eliminating (or at least understanding) the latter will be of significant help.

There is a short chapter on how to be business-minded as a trader. This is a business, and it's crucial that we approach trading with a business frame of mind.

Finally I discuss position management and discipline — the two topics go hand in hand. My approach is more proactive and less mechanical than many, but I believe that we need to adopt a flexible approach based on looking forward rather than backwards.

Chapter 4
Knowledge

In this chapter...

I outline the knowledge that traders require in order to become sustainable and profitable. Gathering knowledge is not a one-off mission; it's something that good traders continue throughout their journey as new markets and ideas develop.

Over the past few years, when I have presented to groups of private traders I have often asked a few questions to gauge the level of knowledge of attendees. One of the consistent themes is a lack of what I would consider to be basic knowledge. For example, typically only around 5 per cent of retail traders that I have questioned have a basic understanding of bonds — yet over 90 per cent can correctly identify a head and shoulders pattern. The financial junk-food industry has done a poor job of educating new traders with real knowledge, and has instead taught unreliable short cuts. I have continually encountered a view among private traders that they do not need in-depth knowledge — that's for the professionals to learn — and their job is just to follow the herd. This is both simplistic and dangerous.

I strongly believe that every trader should try to educate themselves to the highest possible level. You may not become a professional or investment bank trader, but you should at least try to gain the knowledge required. If we are to enjoy a sustainable trading career that encompasses the four core points highlighted earlier, then knowledge will be a key ingredient. Further, in order to become an independent thinker and a trader who doesn't rely on or refer to other people's views, we have to educate ourselves.

Do not expect this to be an overnight process. Take your time to learn as much as possible before you start trading. Graduate trainees at investment banks spend several months learning about all aspects of the business. Interestingly, and importantly, they typically learn each different area from a specialist in that area — so they learn about trading from a trader; they won't have an analyst teaching them to trade. As we will see, even aspects such as stock borrow (the process of borrowing shares in order to settle a short equity trade) and settlement of trades can influence our trading. Further, as markets continue to evolve and new markets and products are created, we need to treat the education process as ongoing. So let's examine what areas of knowledge are required.

Markets

It doesn't matter what market, product or contract we choose to trade; we will all require an understanding of as many markets as possible. Broad knowledge helps us to understand the context of the current trading environment and, as I will explain, also plays an essential role in overcoming some of the heuristics through our watchlists. We cannot build good, comprehensive watchlists without knowledge of many different markets.

Obviously, this book is not the forum for me to explain each of the markets in detail. What I will do is outline the basics of what you need to learn. Fortunately, in the age of Google, finding out the information required is relatively straightforward; just take care to use a reputable, reliable source of information. Even better, seek out some quality books.

Shares

Shares and share markets are typically the products that most of us have exposure to first. We need to understand the drivers of the share markets, common data and valuation methods and also how the main participants operate. Common concepts that we need to understand include:

- P/E ratios
- dividends and dividend yields
- Earnings Per Share (EPS)
- Return on Equity (RoE)
- quick and current ratios
- company debt
- cash flow.

Even if you want to trade FX or commodity futures, you should still learn at least some of these fundamentals about shares; you will see the importance as we progress. P/E ratios and dividend yield, for example, can provide an idea of whether a stock is cheap or expensive, whether they might be in a bull or bear market, and the sentiment of share market participants.

It is impossible to make a good judgement about one particular stock or the overall share market without an understanding of some or all of the items listed above. We are trying to gauge the sentiment of the market and what is being priced into the market. As you will see when I examine watchlists, we need to look at more than one stock and more than one share market in order to make judgements, as one in isolation may not tell us the whole story.

We need to understand how the market and its participants work, because this too can provide important context. For example, with share markets we must understand that the vast majority of participants only trade from the long side; that is, they only buy shares. This is important to know because it means that the tendency is for share traders and investors to be optimistic. Very few (less than 5 per cent typically) ever short sell (sell expecting the price to fall). We will see that this differs from other markets. Markets where it is either difficult to short sell or where most participants don't short sell are the ones that typically are most likely to show overexuberance. We don't tend to expect or see bubbles in dollar–yen or sterling–dollar, but we can see them in shares and the housing market. Expanding on this point, with shares we also need to know that small-cap and some mid-cap shares may not have stock borrow available (that is, we cannot short sell the shares because we cannot borrow stock).

Many private traders and investors do not know the process of short selling, so I will briefly explain it here. It is an important part of the mechanics of our markets, and if you trade shares you need to understand this. If you believe that the price of a share will fall you can profit from selling it at the current price and then buying back at the lower price after the fall (assuming you are correct); that is, you actually sell shares that you don't own. You might ask, though, 'How can settlement of the trade occur if I sell shares that I don't actually own; what do I supply to the buyer?' The answer is that we can only short sell if we can borrow the shares and use these borrowed shares to settle the trade with the buyer.

Typically we borrow from long-term investors, such as managed funds, who lend us the shares for a fee, usually a small percentage. We use these borrowed shares to settle the trade and then as soon as we close out the short trade we can return the borrowed stock back to the lender. If any corporate actions, such as dividend payments, occur during the time we have sold the stock then we must compensate the lender.

Note that the lender (for example, the fund manager) has not sold their shares; they have just lent them to us for settlement purposes. It is important to know that the lender can usually recall the borrowed stock at any time. When stock borrow is recalled from many short-sellers simultaneously, we can see a sharp rise in the share price as the short-sellers then need to buy back the shares; they can only maintain a short position while they have stock borrow in place. On some exchanges it can be possible to sell shares on margin or via other methods and I would encourage you to investigate this process for the market you trade. For bank and hedge fund equity traders, the stock borrow process is part of their basic knowledge and is also an integral factor in their trading and decision making. It is one area where their knowledge gives them edge over the private trader.

So, returning to small-cap and some mid-cap stocks and the unavailability of stock borrow, this means that they often cannot be short sold, and therefore their prices cannot reflect the true beliefs of all participants; they can only reflect the views of those who are positive. If I am bearish on such a stock I cannot enter a position that reflects my view. They are therefore even more prone to strong upward moves, but also can be prone to significant and quick falls if and when the optimistic views are not confirmed by earnings or other news.

This type of information is of particular use for share traders, but there is no reason why traders of other products should not be aware as well. If you are trading these types of shares, though, it's imperative that you understand how the market operates and what the price really reflects. The concept that 'everything is in the price', which is accepted by many traders, economists and technical analysts, is simply not true for many small- and mid-cap shares. This needs to be included in our decision making.

Hopefully, you now understand that knowing how the market operates is a crucial part of our knowledge, a fact that is often overlooked by retail traders. I can say that bank and hedge-fund traders are very aware of these issues and do incorporate them into their decision making. Share traders need to understand that large cap stocks are very different from small caps, and each requires the weighing up of different information.

This is the type of information we need to understand about shares and companies in general. If you decide to trade shares, then you should learn some of the more in-depth concepts—but even if you are trading a different market it'll still be worth your while gathering some of this knowledge, otherwise you will find the construction and implementation of watchlists more difficult. Note, too, that I have also investigated the actual mechanics of the market, in particular here the process of short selling.

Whatever market you trade, it is vital that you understand how the market actually works and incorporate that into your trading. This is typically a major failing of retail traders. My decision making and analysis of stocks where there is no borrow available, and therefore no short positions, is different from ones that can be short sold.

However, we also need to understand that, in general, and compared to some other markets, very few participants in the share market ever short sell, so it's a market that can be prone to exuberance and, subsequently, disappointment. Understanding and embracing this idea will help when we investigate the topic of 'pricing in' later on.

Foreign exchange (FX)

FX (currency) markets are generally more straightforward than shares (as long as you keep away from the more obscure cross rates). There are roughly half a dozen core cross rates that are the main ones to trade, plus a further couple of dozen or so smaller cross rates that are often just proxies for the core rates. It is generally believed that currencies are driven by macroeconomic events and data, so these are areas that all FX traders need to understand. I will cover them shortly.

There is no doubt that FX is currently the flavour of the month for retail traders. Having been burned by the junk-food industry on futures and CFDs, retail traders are now being told that the liquid and 24-hour currency markets hold the key to profitability. My own view is that it's not the market or product that has hurt retail traders; it's the techniques and analysis that they use. It doesn't matter what you trade; if your techniques and knowledge are poor, you are more likely to lose.

There are a couple of important points to realise about FX markets, as they carry great significance to short-term traders. With the FX process we typically do not have access to a reliable order book (the list of buy and sell orders), and most retail traders see no trading price. This is because there is not one market or price for a currency cross rate; they are traded at different locations at the same time at slightly different prices. For short-term traders in particular this means that we see far less information than we can access for other products, such as exchange-traded futures.

The major FX rates are among the most liquid markets in the world and, unlike with shares, there is no difference between buying and selling a rate (that is, there are no issues around having to borrow in order to sell; we can sell the dollar–yen rate as easily as buying it). This means that the markets are typically more reflective of everyone's views. While with shares we saw that a vast majority of participants only trade from the long side (around 95 per cent), this of course is not the case for currencies.

The spread of positions and types of traders is also very different. Some players in FX markets are only using the product to hedge currency risk exposure. For example, a US firm that generates significant income from the eurozone will have exposure to the euro–dollar rate and may wish to protect itself from some of this risk. Central banks can also participate in currency markets from time to time, usually to stem volatility or try to stop a particularly strong move. The corporate hedger and central bank are generally not part of the share market, so that is a difference between these two markets.

Of course we will never know when and to what degree the corporate hedgers are trading, but nonetheless part of our background knowledge is to understand who trades our markets and how they go about their trading. Every market is different, despite what many (particularly technical analysts) tell us. We cannot adopt the same analysis for each market; if you trade FX you will need to weigh up different situations than a share trader will. Hence the first thing we must do is find out how our market works and who the main players are.

Again, I have provided only a flavour of the FX market. For more information there are some good books available, but this is also an area where a good broker can help. Brokers at decent-sized institutions will be able to inform you of the various flows and customer types, because their institution should see a variety of customers. I don't expect them to provide names, but accurate (first-hand) information about what type of customer is doing what can be useful to us, particularly in a market where we don't actually see any trade information on screen.

Bonds

A lack of knowledge about bond markets is typically a key failing of retail traders. Whether you trade bonds or bond futures or not, you should learn about and understand bond markets. They too are among the largest and most liquid markets in the world. There are basically two types of bonds: corporate bonds and government bonds. Corporate bonds are issued by companies as a way of raising capital, while government bonds are issued by governments (through their central bank) to finance a government's activities and debt.

The prices of both corporate and government bonds will rise and fall depending on a number of factors, including inflation expectations and also the market's sentiment towards that particular company or country. So tracking bond markets can provide us with useful information about expectations about a company or country, and companies and economies in general. As I explain in chapter 5, all of this information is crucial to us.

Bonds are quoted in terms of both a price and the yield that the price reflects. This is not the forum for a full and thorough explanation of bond prices, and I would encourage you to read further on this. In simple terms, if a bond price rises, its yield will fall; this may reflect a number of situations that include falling inflation expectations or an improved outlook for the particular company or country.

For government bonds we also need to look at the shape of the yield curve; this is essentially the difference between short-term yields and longer term ones. In addition to the individual yield movements, the relationship between short-term and long-term rates (known as the yield curve) can also provide us with information. For example if long-term rates are lower than short-term yields (referred to as an inverted yield curve) it typically reflects a view among bond traders that the economy will slow, leading to the future cutting of interest rates. Inverse yield curves have been reasonable indicators of slowing economies and recession — but, as with any indicator, we must not base a judgement on one only.

Gathering information on corporate bonds can be more difficult for private traders, but there are increasing opportunities on the internet to do so. Good sources of financial market data, such as Bloomberg, can provide information on corporate bond activity.

Another source of data on corporate bonds is the credit default swap (CDS) market. CDSs are essentially insurance products for bonds; if the price rises, it typically reflects increased nervousness about the company (or country, for sovereign CDS). Falling CDS prices usually occur in periods of stability. So for example, during the GFC, CDS prices rose sharply, while during the more stable markets of 2013 they have generally fallen. Some CDS indices (groups of corporate CDSs) can be found on the internet, with the firm Markit being a good source of data. Again I would imagine that CDSs are a new product to most readers, but they can offer us some useful information. Spending an hour or so researching some more about them will be time well spent. When I started trading, CDSs did not exist — but as they started to trade more heavily I obviously needed to learn more about them. This is an example of how we need to keep abreast of new markets and the information they can offer.

Commodities

Commodities are typically grouped into precious metals, industrial metals, energy and soft commodities. Obviously if you choose to trade one of these markets (usually through futures) then I would suggest you conduct as much due diligence and research as possible. As with the other markets, each of these commodity markets will have different participants, and some markets will have different seasonality effects and settlement and warehousing processes. You should aim to fully understand your market before trading it, as settlement, delivery and similar issues can affect trading.

Even those of us who do not usually trade commodities will still need to follow the major commodity markets and so we will require some knowledge of them. Commodities trade in the spot market (today's price for the physical commodity), the forward market (future price for the physical commodity) and futures markets. I would suggest that it's easier for retail traders to get data from the futures market while checking news coming from the physical markets as well. I demonstrate the use of this data in chapter 5.

Once you have built up your knowledge of markets, the next step is to investigate their relationship with each other. It is important to remember that no correlation or relationship between any two markets is ever set in stone, but we can investigate what each market is pricing in and then work out if there are inconsistencies. We look at this further in chapter 5.

Derivatives

I want to quickly discuss derivatives because these are often a misunderstood, misrepresented and misused product in the retail trading business. You will not be surprised to learn that much of this misinformation stems from the financial junk-food sector. Used correctly, derivatives can add to our trading in different ways. Handled effectively, the leverage that they can provide can be of great use and I demonstrate this clearly in chapter 10. Some derivatives (for example, options) can also offer us more ways to express our trading view: that is, they increase our trading possibilities and can therefore improve our trading. The flip side, of course, is that, used incorrectly, they can cause significant losses. So, as always, research and knowledge is required. It's important to gain knowledge from the right sources, especially as we are dealing with products where poor decisions can be very costly.

With options, for example, I again have a different perspective from the typical financial junk-food view. Typically, retail traders are told to sell options as the preferred method of making money. They are told that most options expire worthless, so it's better to sell them and collect the premium. My view is different, and it goes back to rule number one from the start of this part of the book: preserve our capital. I have seen too many traders lose substantial amounts, sometimes substantially more than their trading capital, through selling options. As a result it's a strategy that I rarely, if ever, employ when I trade with my own capital.

Through using options, though, even just long option strategies, I can greatly improve my trading. For example, for a typical retail trader who might be bullish on a stock, the only way he can express his view is to buy that stock. However, using a knowledge of options I would also be able to consider buying call options, or a call spread or call butterfly, and I would have a range of strike prices and expiries to examine. Typically I would look through at least a couple of dozen different strategies, each offering different risk/reward/expected return, and each would work differently in different market conditions. I could therefore find the right strategy to fit with my view, risk profile and time frame. It is possible through options to find trades with better risk/reward profiles than simply buying the underlying (shares in this case), and with a much smaller initial outlay. It might be that I end up simply buying the shares, but the point is that, through a knowledge of options, I can expand the trade opportunities available and improve my trading and profitability.

Here is just an example of how increased knowledge and an understanding and correct implementation of derivatives can help our trading. Being a share trader (or currency or commodity trader) who only trades shares is like being a golfer who only uses one of his irons; no matter how well you use it you're not playing to your potential, and there will be times when your tool is not sufficient.

If we go back to the core rule number 2 — we must be able to trade in as many market conditions as possible — you should see that being able to use derivatives such as options correctly is essential. There are times, particularly when volatility is at extremes (very high or very low) that options can and will offer better trades than the underlying contract. 'Put options' offer the ability to express a bearish view on the contract and again, through different put option strategies, they can offer a variety of ways to express the view. Remember that at all times here I am assuming trades where we buy options so we have a defined, maximum downside and sometimes unlimited upside potential. Of course, if the contract that you trade does not have options (or other derivatives) that are easily tradeable (good liquidity and tight bid/offer spreads) then your trading possibilities will be limited.

Derivatives such as options can also play another crucial role in our trading (and for investors too) in that they can be excellent tools for hedging a position. We may have a trade that we are comfortable with on the whole, but perhaps there is some data coming up and, rather than exit the trade, we can choose to create a hedge trade. Again, the concept of hedging will be new to many readers but it is routinely practised among professional traders. Hedging is where we establish an opposing trade to the one we have, to offset some or all of the directional risk. Understanding how to hedge a position is another skill that will help you to trade in more market conditions and is particularly useful in times of volatility.

For example, let's say that we are long some gold shares that correlate quite strongly with the gold price. We're approaching some economic data and we're aware that there is a possibility of some movement in the price of gold possibly related to US-dollar movement. A trader who only understands and trades shares really only has three choices: to sell all the position, sell some of the position or to carry the risk and keep the whole position.

Now, if I'm a more knowledgeable share trader and I understand related derivatives and hedging techniques, I can also examine a range of other possibilities. These include selling gold futures, buying put options on gold futures, and buying put option strategies on my shares (if available); furthermore, these put option ideas will have a range of alternatives. The result of this knowledge is that I will be able to examine dozens of alternatives and can select the one that offers the risk protection that I want at the cost that I'm willing to pay. I have a much greater chance of finding a good trade and, over time, a much greater chance of trading through these occasions.

So this one simple example shows the benefits of knowledge, in this case both of derivatives and hedging techniques. A simple share trader would have far fewer trading alternatives, and is therefore likely at times to carry too much risk (and possibly at times to exit trades that could have been carried with a hedge).

There are other issues that we need to understand when using derivatives. I suggest that CFDs and futures should only be used for short-term trading; that is, I would not advise using them for trades that could exist for a few weeks. For such longer term (by trader standards) trades I believe that options can offer a better alternative. There are a number of reasons for this view, but in short, products with significant leverage and the potential for significant downside (such as futures) can exhibit stronger swings both in terms of price movement and margin requirement and therefore can be difficult to hold for such time frames. Long option positions can be subject to fewer margin swings (some require full upfront payment and therefore no further margin) and so they can be easier positions to hold over a longer time frame. CFDs are subject to funding costs, which can mount up over a longer time frame. Holding significant leverage, therefore, should only be done over the very short term.

An understanding of derivatives such as options, and also hedging skills, does not come overnight—but this is knowledge that we should all aim to build up over time. This is knowledge that all of the best bank and hedge-fund traders have, and it gives them significant edge over most retail traders. Returning to the four core trading principles from the start of the chapter, the knowledge and skills that derivatives and hedging offer us directly support at least three of the four: they help to preserve capital, trade in different market conditions and they slow down our decision making so that we are making more informed decisions.

Short-selling shares

For readers who plan to trade shares, the techniques of short selling will be vital to understand. I have already approached the topic in this chapter, but here I want to explain why successful traders need to be able to short sell. Again I refer to the core principles—in this case the important ones are preserving capital and being able to trade in different market conditions. If you decide to trade shares (and by 'trade' I mean short-term positions, not long-term investments) and you only trade from the long side (that is, you only buy shares) then you will be unable to trade during times when shares are falling; you are eliminating great trading opportunities. Later in this chapter I will explain my preference for specialisation—if you are to follow this advice, then you will need to be able to short sell.

Earlier I explained how traders need to be independent thinkers who will sometimes take contrarian views. Short-selling shares is an expression of this. Having traded through a number of occasions when stock markets were falling sharply, I can state that, were it not for short selling, I would not have survived.

With the issues around stock borrow discussed earlier in this chapter, and also because it's a technique that's probably out of the comfort zone for most retail traders, I do not expect everyone to embrace this immediately. As with everything I suggest, take your time learning about it and then practise using a demonstration account, or even paper trading, before you trade for real. When you trade against the herd you must be nimble and disciplined and you need to understand the risks. But similarly, there are times when the information at hand tells us to be short, and so we should be able to do so.

If you understand options then it can also be possible to express a short position through buying a put option strategy, and this can be a viable alternative without the borrowing implications; again, though, it requires knowledge. I should also say that it can be very hard to run short equity positions for any substantial length of time; with most share market participants trading from the long side only, we are likely to be stopped out after a few days (assuming we are using a trailing stop, as explained later). It can be easier to short sell a stock a number of times than try to hold the short position for the duration of a long-term fall.

Short selling has a bad reputation in the retail industry, in the media in particular. It is often said that short-sellers are performing some kind of almost evil act, and some have even called for it to be banned. I completely disagree and wrote in more depth about my views in an article in *YourTradingEdge* magazine a few years ago. A number of commentators had made the point that short-sellers drive share prices too low, which is damaging to investors. I would counter that share investors, being long-term holders, will not be damaged by being able to buy shares that are too low; share investors lose money when they buy shares that are too expensive. Thus the real damage is done by those on the sell side who sell them overpriced shares.

My own view is that one of the reasons for share prices that are too high, and the subsequent sharp crashes or corrections, is that there are too few short-sellers. If a share price is overvalued, which obviously can happen, then what is wrong with someone expressing their opinion of this by short selling it? Why is it okay for someone to buy an overvalued stock, but not to sell it? In a true market we should all be free to express our views. It will not help investors in the long run to ban short selling, as they will only end up buying shares that are even more overpriced. The hedge funds that short sell only do so after significant analysis, and I would suggest it's better for investors to watch these players; perhaps they're alerting the market to an overpriced stock. If so, they're doing the market and investors a favour.

Given the controversy around short selling it is important for those who practise it to remember that during times of extreme volatility, institutions and exchanges have placed curbs and even stopped short selling entirely. Such actions result in severe rallies (called short squeezes) that will obviously hurt short positions, so we need to factor this into our thinking.

In normal market conditions short selling can be fine, but in extreme times using put options is the better trade. It's all part of using the right trade at the right time. My suggestion is, if in doubt use the conservative trade — preservation first.

Data

All markets are affected by the release of data, and the suggestion by many in the financial junk-food industry that you don't need to understand the various pieces of data is plain wrong. I believe that the widely held view that markets are ahead is incorrect. This is a big call to make, seeing as this theory underpins some aspects of Efficient Market Hypothesis and technical analysis, but that is the judgement that I make based on my experience of trading. My alternative suggestion is that markets price in information; that is, participants make judgements about what they *expect* to happen; they don't know what *will* happen. The role of data is crucial because it is when data is released that participants find out whether they are right. This is why we can get such severe moves from markets after the release of data.

I will discuss the concept of pricing in more depth in chapter 8, but for the time being the important point to accept is that data is important and it does move markets. As traders wanting to build a sustainable career, it's vital that we understand as much as possible about anything that can affect the price of the contract we're trading and related contracts. An understanding of data, including when it is released, will greatly help our assessment of possible future outcomes (another crucial part of our decision making that I will explain later). In short, we cannot make decent trading decisions without knowledge of the various data that hits our markets.

There are various pieces of data; some are more macro-economic, some are stock-specific and others are related to specific markets. I will outline a few.

Macro-economic

We should all have at least a basic understanding of what these data are and how they could affect the market we trade. This is clearly not an exhaustive list, but this should certainly be the starting point. Different countries release slightly different variants and sometimes different pieces of economic data. Information on all is easily available on the web, as are calendars showing when they are to be released and what analysts' expectations are. The key data to study are:

- GDP
- retail sales
- inflation
- unemployment
- consumer and business sentiment figures
- industrial production.

Stock specific

On a daily basis there can be many forms of company news and announcements. These include:

- company earnings
- corporate actions, for example, takeovers, mergers, stock splits and so on.

Market specific

These are just some examples of market-specific data to look out for:

- bond auctions
- oil inventories
- weather events (for agricultural commodities).

Part of the due diligence process for trading is to find out what data affects the market we have chosen to trade, and which ones tend to produce the biggest reaction.

Specialisation

As traders we require edge over other participants if we are to make consistent profits. That edge can come from a number of sources, including our discipline and knowledge. We don't need to have edge over every other market participant, but we need to have edge over some of them. I'm the first to admit that it's hard for retail traders to gain edge over bank traders, given that the latter see far more trades and flow. But knowing that so many retail traders use poor analysis and trading techniques, there can be profit to be made from having edge over that group alone. Also, trading for a shorter time frame can also provide edge over the many participants who trade with a longer term outlook, even if these are professionals. In fact, the 'bread and butter' for many bank traders' profits is trading in and out of the flow of business from longer term fund managers.

One significant way that we can gain edge over other participants is to specialise; that is, trade one contract (or sector, for share traders). I have already mentioned this in chapter 1, but it's worth including here too. When you specialise you gain a better understanding of how the participants in your market operate and how they react to information. This will help you judge risk and reward and should also help your entry and exits from trades.

While over the last few pages I have introduced more work and information for you to gather, by specialising it actually becomes easier to do this. When you look at the same information and the same contract day after day, it will become second nature, and over time a market that looked complex and perhaps even overwhelming when you started will become clearer to you. It won't become easy (because trading never is) but, as I explained with the story about the Gilt trader in chapter 1, it's easier to make decisions about something that you look at every day rather than a contract that you have never, or rarely, traded before.

FX traders should look to trade one cross rate while of course monitoring the others. As most of the active rates involve the US dollar, trading more than one makes less sense anyway, because you could essentially just have the same US dollar position two or three times — just against different cross currencies. The cross rates that you do not trade will provide information for the one that you do.

Similarly, futures traders should specialise in one contract in the same way that those wily old floor traders used to. Being specialists by trading in one futures pit each and every day gave the floor traders huge edge over the majority non-specialist futures traders.

For those who want to trade shares, the situation is slightly different. Specialising in one stock may not provide many opportunities and is impractical. Share traders should therefore specialise in a sector, selecting around half-a-dozen stocks in that sector. When you decide to take a position it will be in one, perhaps two of the stocks if the trades are the same direction. For example, if you are looking at six gold shares and want to take a long position, it's unwise to buy all of the six stocks — you should take position in just one or two that you believe offer the best trade. If you want to enter long and short trades at the same time then you might have positions in more than two. As your knowledge increases over time it can be possible to research and then start trading a second sector, but this is not essential — and if you find that trading another sector actually harms your trading, then go back to your initial setup.

You may have been surprised to learn that most bank traders are specialists, but that is indeed the case: they are also generally very short-term traders. Both of these strategies provide edge for them and I strongly believe that they offer advantages to retail traders too. Try to become an expert in something rather than a jack of all trades and master of none.

Summary

- Knowledge of markets and data is required.
- Specialists have more knowledge than others in their market, which provides edge.
- Both knowledge and specialisation help us to understand context.

Chapter 5

Watchlists

In this chapter...

I explain how to prepare and use watchlists, one of the most important information-gathering tools for a trader.

Collecting information is crucial to traders, but it's an area that so many fail in. If you collect bad information or the wrong type of information (noise) then your trading will suffer; this is the case for many private traders in particular. It's not just a case of 'the more, the better'—it's the quality of information that matters, and how we apply it. So before I begin to explain how to build watchlists I first need to explain the difference between information (which we need) and noise (which we don't).

Information and noise

To understand the difference between information and noise, it's perhaps easier to start by understanding the latter. Noise is the opposite of factual or reliable information, so it would include rumours or even a particular person's views. 'Noise traders', as defined by Fisher Black, are traders who trade on such evidence in the belief that it provides edge. I believe that technical analysis traders are also a significant group of noise traders, as the evidence shows that using chart patterns and indicators is unlikely to lead to profitability for most. Indeed, a research piece about the head-and-shoulders pattern by the New York Federal Reserve referred to those who used the pattern as noise traders because they used it in the belief it would generate profits, while in reality it was unreliable.

To draw a line between noise and information, I classify information as being data direct from the market. It's how the markets are actually moving, rather than people's long-term views. While it's true that market prices also contain noise (because many market participants are far from rational or knowledgeable), they are our only source of information about what participants are actually doing. Further, by bringing in information from a wide range of markets we can improve the information that we are seeing, as I will explain later in this chapter.

To explain the difference between noise and information, here are a few examples.

> A broker or analyst appears on TV and states that China will continue to buy base metals as its economy grows, and he is therefore bullish on iron ore miners over the medium term.

This is noise. We are hearing a view of a sell side individual, and analysts are often very wrong in their forecasts. Private traders place too much emphasis on this type of broker/analyst noise.

> The price of iron ore is rising.

This is information, as it's the price itself, not someone's view of it. Importantly, we can only make good judgements of how it's performing at the current time; just because it's rallying now does not mean it will rally for a longer period. (That would be applying the representative bias of taking a small amount of data and extrapolating beyond its true value.) We would then want to seek other information related to iron ore — perhaps the cost of shipping it, or the price of steel, which of course is related to iron ore.

> While current economic growth is weak, an analyst states that Country X will see significant growth next year due to a range of factors.

This is noise—again, it's the view of one person. This industry contains millions of people's views—if we listen to them all, we'll get conflicting suggestions. Not all of these people are active market participants; some are sell side individuals so we should ignore them and focus on what the markets are really doing. These views are based on many assumptions, and for traders assumptions are dangerous.

> While current economic growth is weak, the yield curve of Country X has in recent weeks moved from having an inverted shape to a regular, positive slope.

This is information—bond market participants are now pricing in a more positive outlook, and we can then use this information to see if other markets agree or not. Bond markets are typically very large, and for changes such as this to occur there needs to be a change of view among many participants. Further, without 'mum and dad' investors and permanently bullish fund managers, brokers and analysts, bond markets can often be a more reliable source of information.

There are significant benefits from cutting out noise: it obviously saves time, but it also simplifies our thought process. Freeing ourselves from the constant stream of views and opinions is actually liberating. We no longer care what a particular analyst or journalist thinks about a stock or a market; we'll only look at the market itself. So while building knowledge about a wide range of markets is time-consuming to begin with, it will actually save us time over the long run. We will no longer rely on the views of others; we will rely on our own knowledge. Traders need to think for themselves, and doing so requires knowledge—which in turn helps us to cut out noise.

The role of watchlists

Watchlists are central to the collection of information, and the start of our analysis and trading decisions. They must therefore be constructed with care so that they assist our ability to make objective decisions. Built correctly, they can help us to overcome some of the biases and provide us with trade ideas and alert us to changes in sentiment. They can also save time by helping to eliminate noise.

Rather than simply tell you what to put into a watchlist, I'll explain the core principles behind constructing watchlists. It's important for you to understand why the watchlists are constructed as they are, so that you can build your own and improve on them over time. Later in the chapter, I will show an example of one type of watchlist.

The importance of following different markets

In the last chapter I explained that, no matter what market we actually trade, we need to have an understanding of as many different markets and contracts as possible. There are some very good reasons for doing so, both in terms of building our knowledge of the overall market context, and also in helping to overcome some of the heuristics (short cuts) that we are prone to. The basic knowledge outlined in the previous chapter is a necessity if we are to correctly implement watchlists and achieve these two goals of understanding context and avoiding some short cuts.

Contrary to accepted wisdom, I don't believe that the price of any contract reflects all available information. The belief that 'everything is in the price' is a fundamental assumption of technical analysis and is widely accepted by even fundamental traders (traders who use traditional fundamental analysis) too. Sometimes, though, market mechanics mean that it cannot be possible for everything to be in the price. For example, with small-cap stocks, the lack of stock borrow leads to bearish traders being unable to act. We know that a vast majority of share market participants only ever trade from the long side, so again this can lead to a distorted picture — overoptimism can abound among share market participants. As discussed previously, bond and currency markets have different participants, while commodity markets have a completely different set of traders again.

Sometimes different markets price in different expectations. While in chapter 8 I will discuss the concept of pricing in, it relates to the fact that market participants price in information, as opposed to the belief that the markets are ahead and that traders know what will happen. This concept is based on my experience of trading at the heart of many markets, and is central to my analysis and trading. So by looking at a range of different markets we can see if all markets are pricing in similar views, or if there are differences. This will help us to both identify new trades and make decisions on existing ones.

For example, I have seen many occasions when share markets have rallied, yet bond markets have also rallied, with a flattening bias on the yield curve. The latter suggests that economic activity might be slowing and so can be a contrary position to the bullish nature of the share market. We do not know which market is right (this will be found out later) but we at least now know that there are different views. If we only looked at share prices, we would not get this information. Similarly, you might find that the local currency was falling sharply, which again could indicate nervousness about that country that is contrary to the exuberance of the share traders.

Looking at only one market or type of product will only provide information from that type of market. So it's crucial for us to get information from a number of sources and examine what a range of different participants are thinking. This is a vitally important part of our analysis—do not assume that your market or the participants in your market are pricing in what everyone else is. In fact, if I were to ask private share traders and investors whether they use bond market information in their analysis, I would estimate that in excess of 90 per cent would say 'no'. This would add further proof to the view that not everything is being priced into markets.

Share markets are possibly the worst in this regard, due to the fact that most participants only ever trade from the long side. Saying that, don't assume that currency markets or bond markets are always more reflective of available information; no matter what market or product you trade, take your information from a wide variety of other markets in order to make better judgements. While I believe, for example, that in general bond markets are better indicators than share markets, this does not mean they are always right.

Using watchlists to help overcome biases

I have explained that confirmation bias is the tendency for people to seek views that agree with their own, or to overweight information that confirms their view and underweight or disregard contrarian information. It's undoubtedly a bias that's evident among traders and investors (and brokers and analysts), and so we need to find ways to overcome it. One of our aims when making trading decisions is to remain as objective as possible, and obviously confirmation bias can prevent this.

In order to overcome confirmation bias we need to actively seek out disconfirming information; that is, we need to look for information that does not agree with our view, or is contrary to what we might be seeing from our market. If we do not find such information then we can proceed with the trade or enter a trade based on the information we have collected, but we must constantly re-evaluate the information and keep looking for the disconfirming evidence. If or when we find disconfirming evidence we need to decide whether to exit the trade, reduce it or hedge it. The key point, though, is to actively seek out reasons why we might be wrong.

I know that this can sound odd to many people, and indeed at one trading desk that I worked on I was sometimes thought of as lacking self-belief (and sometimes as just plain awkward) because I was always looking for reasons why we might be wrong; but the fact is that in order to be ahead of others in our market (to gain edge) we need to find information that they may not see. We need to find out why we might be wrong, because it's losses that will hurt us—if we're right, then profits take care of themselves. Referring back to the core principles at the start of this section, preservation of our capital is vital if we are to stay in this business for any length of time. Looking for disconfirming evidence is clearly a way to overcome confirmation bias, and helps us to make better decisions. I would say that this discipline is one that is practised by very few traders and investors, yet with a well-constructed watchlist it's not difficult to employ. The scientific method is based on the idea that the only way to prove a theory is to try and disprove it. No amount of confirming information will prove a theory, but only one piece of disconfirming information can disprove it.

Our watchlists play a vital role because they contain the views of many different participants from a range of different markets. We are more likely to find disconfirming evidence if we look at different markets than if we just analyse our own market. Share traders will typically look at share indices and various stock prices to gauge a view of market sentiment. However, this is a form of confirmation bias—generally bullish individuals looking at what other bullish individuals are thinking. Similarly, traders of one US dollar cross rate will be watching how other US dollar rates are faring—again, as these are all linked and traded by similar participants. While this does provide us with some information, it doesn't allow us to see the whole picture.

At times in our career we will need to take the opposite position to others in our market; sometimes what others have priced in will be proved wrong. So seeking evidence that they might be wrong is crucial. Sure, in the very short term if the US dollar is falling against most of its counterparts then it may be more likely to fall in the one we are trading—but what if other US dollar assets are starting to rally? We may want to position differently.

Once you have constructed your watchlist, the actual process of looking at all markets on it each day should be relatively straightforward. The difficulty comes with whether you have the discipline to act on what you see; this is where, for some, trading becomes too difficult. Rather like facing up to cutting a losing position quickly, acting on what you see can be easier said than done.

This is where conservativeness comes in, the tendency for people to cling to an opinion. The first step to overcome this is to seek different opinions, which we are hopefully all doing with our new watchlists. The next step is to act on that information; to have the ability to change your mind when the facts change. I'm not sure whether this can be taught; it's a potential demon that we all must overcome by ourselves.

Understanding context can also assist with overcoming another bias, hindsight bias. As I explained in chapter 2, hindsight bias is the tendency for people, post-event, to believe that they could have known the outcome pre-event. We cannot learn from the past unless we understand how those past events unfolded, and this requires an understanding of the context for those events. As I have already explained, charts and historical data alone cannot help us to know why the instrument traded as it did. The Winter Olympic speed skating final won by Steven Bradbury is a great example of why context is so important, and why hindsight bias needs to be eliminated. So far, to my knowledge, real-time context and analysis is the only way to achieve this.

Trade the markets

The point about acting on what we see is a topic that I would like to investigate a little further. When trading, the objective is to be objective; we need to trade the markets, not our beliefs or the beliefs of others. From experience working with many traders, I know that this is easier said than done. I hope that dispensing with a belief system such as using chart patterns might be quite easy to do once you understand that they are unreliable. However, I imagine that all traders and investors have their own views on macro issues: what the economy is going to do and which companies they like and dislike.

It's perfectly reasonable to expect that we all have opinions on these types of topics. The problems come with using these opinions as a basis for trading. Typically these views may be more long term, but we also have to recognise when they are based on information and when they are simply our opinion. For example, there are many traders who hold a macro view that the current low interest rate and loose monetary policy of many central banks will lead to high inflation and higher gold prices. Indeed there are many commentators making big names for themselves with such views (these types of big calls are popular on TV and for quotes in articles). But as (short term) traders we cannot allow such views to cloud our objective decision making. We must trade the markets, not our views — and that involves making decisions based on information. Sure, if the information shows that gold is rising, inflation is rising, and so on, then we can start to trade that view — but until or unless that happens, we cannot trade that view. Indeed, 2013 was a very hard year of big losses for those who traded that particular view of gold and inflation.

I'm sure that some of you are thinking, 'But surely trading is about taking views on what will happen—isn't that what Soros and other big players do?' The answer is yes and no, but for us, predominantly no. It is true that some hedge fund managers do make such calls, but the better ones still base their decision on information (I recommend Soros's books as good guides and sources). Timing is always important for traders, because if our timing is out then we are likely to get stopped out of a position (at a loss). If you trade one of these macro-type views, then you need to have very deep pockets—and that goes against the discipline that traders need.

It's common for private traders to believe that trading is all about making these big macro calls—after all, the sell side, which is so dominant in the media, is constantly making these calls. However, for most professional traders I have encountered and traded alongside, trading is about short-term decisions; picking up small amounts of money, but doing so regularly and compounding profits.

It's rare for the big macro calls to come true, so we're better off keeping them as opinions in the same way that most sports fans have lots of views about their sport, but rarely place bets on those views. I would imagine that the majority of sports fans who do bet on their views lose money. As I explain in chapter 10, I would rather try to operate as the bookmaker, trading in and out of market activity, than as a punter. Trading macro views is akin to being a punter, and that is not where we should be aiming. Remember, too, that working out risk and reward for these longer term views is far more difficult than for short-term trades—so they involve a larger degree of risk too.

Personally, if I wish to express a longer term view I will do so through buying an option strategy—but only if I can find one that offers good risk/reward. That way I can limit my downside, spend a relatively small amount of money for good potential upside, and the position can sit aside from my day-to-day trading without affecting what I do.

It is important, as traders, that we don't allow the macro views to cloud our day-to-day trading. For example, if you're a short-term trader of gold futures but you have a longer term macro bullish outlook on gold, you must not let this view interfere with your short-term trading. Otherwise you'll find it hard to short gold futures when the information tells you to do so. This is why being able to make objective decisions based on the philosophy of 'trade what you see' is so important.

Include positively and inversely correlated markets

Some markets are correlated positively — that is, they tend to move in the same direction. For example, we might generally expect the FTSE 100 Index to move in the same direction as the US S&P 500 Index. We might also expect gold to move in the same direction as silver. So we include a few positively correlated markets in our watchlists, as they can provide information to us. However, it's also important to include and investigate inversely correlated markets; that is, markets that tend to move in opposite directions. Examples of these can be bonds and equities, and also gold and the US dollar.

The first point that I want to state here is that no correlation is set in stone, so once again it's important to make no assumptions. However, we can glean significant information if markets that had been correlating inversely start correlating positively (and the same can be said for positively correlating markets that start correlating inversely, although this is less common). For example, if gold had been correlating inversely with the US dollar (US dollar up and gold down, because it's priced in US dollars), then if this were to change and both markets rose together for a sustained period of time, it would suggest that something had changed. This would be information that we would need to investigate further.

The good news for us is that if we have constructed our watchlists properly, using the markets that I suggested in chapter 4, we will have included both positively and inversely correlated markets. In doing so, we have again improved the range of information and perspectives that we are seeing.

Watchlists help us to build context and better understand markets

At the start of every day, our first task is to look at our watchlists; rather than look at what people are saying about what has happened overnight, we will look at what has actually occurred. If we see some big moves then we will investigate further—perhaps some data came out or something unexpected happened.

Our watchlists contain information from many markets and many different participants, so by looking at each we can gain a good idea of sentiment among a range of markets and then decide if they agree or not. Therefore our understanding of sentiment and the current context is enhanced. When we enter trades and monitor them we should have an understanding of the current circumstances and, if we continue to objectively use the watchlists, we should also be aware when these circumstances change. Understanding context is a key part of trading analysis, one that many private traders omit because they find it too hard. But if we construct good watchlists it need not be a task that is beyond the capabilities of most.

By referring to good watchlists with a range of different markets each day, you will also build up your understanding of how markets work together, and your understanding of markets in general will improve. If after the previous chapter you started to feel that it was all looking too hard, it might be better to construct a watchlist and start following the markets. Obviously don't trade until or unless you are confident that you can digest and understand what is happening, but the process of following a wide range of markets should improve your understanding. You will likely find that by looking at bond yield curves, credit derivatives and other new markets, the financial world will look very different. You may even see that markets you have traded previously and thought you understood now appear to be very different. For example, share traders might find that occasions when they previously would have been bullish might now look less so because they see different information.

As a result, you may well find there are far fewer trading opportunities than you had previously thought. This is good, because there are almost certainly fewer good opportunities than most private traders, brokers and analysts believe there to be.

Also, don't get caught up in the false belief that we can understand all markets all of the time, or that all price moves can be forecast or predicted in advance. There are times when we cannot fully understand what is happening—in which case, we do nothing. Similarly, we cannot understand or predict every move in every market each day or each week. Certainly, every market may move almost every day, but this does not mean that each of those moves can be traded. Our job is to only trade the moves that we can understand and that are backed by various pieces of information.

A belief in chart reading, trendlines and backtested indicators can lead traders to think that they can find an indicator that allows us to trade all moves—we can't; or rather, we shouldn't. There is an element of randomness to markets and we need to understand that and not always try to find reasons for every move. This last point is essential to grasp; we're not trying to find stories behind every move—we're trying to work out what is going on and trade the moves that we understand and that are backed by information from a variety of sources.

Once you start to watch more markets and try to piece the information together you will further understand why we shouldn't rely on the sell side or media for our information. For example, after a day when shares were modestly higher I saw a headline along the following lines: 'Australia shares rise as risk appetite improves'. On the face of it, it was a regular type of headline that would usually be accepted without concern by most private traders. However, when I looked at my watchlists for the day, the picture that I saw was somewhat different. It was true that the overall share market index had rallied, but when I drilled down into some individual stocks I found that the gainers were blue-chip high-yielding shares, such as the big four banks. Smaller cap shares and more speculative stocks were mixed but many were lower, some quite substantially (more than 2 or 3 per cent). If risk appetite really had improved I would have expected to see riskier shares perform better.

Further, a look at the local bond market showed that bond prices had risen slightly for the day; again contrary to what I would expect if risk appetite was improving. A glance at the Aussie dollar showed that it was flat on the day, not the rally that I would expect on a move to riskier assets. My watchlists told me that there was no theme to the trading day; it was quite a quiet one with no discernible direction. If I had to make a decision as to whether risk assets were in demand or not I would probably suggest that they were not—I had more evidence of safer assets being supported—but again there was no strong information.

The sell side and the media like and need headlines; they like to have a story for every day, every event and every move. We as traders must not be driven down that path—we must only be focused on real information and what is really happening. The headline example has hopefully demonstrated how the world can appear very different to us than it does to the sell side. The first part of the headline, 'Australian shares rise', was correct to a degree (the index was higher) so I would accept that to be information. However, the second part of the headline, 'as risk appetite improves', was simply a story made up to try to explain the rise; it was noise.

Beware stock closing prices

In the first section of the book I explained how closing prices can be influenced by some odd circumstances, and that they can sometimes be poor reflections of the trading day. This is predominantly more the case for shares than it is for others products. For example, FX rates don't really have the same closing mechanics, and most futures markets are almost 24-hour now too. But if you are looking through a share watchlist and see some moves that look odd or out of sync, my first suggestion is to look through the day's trading and see if the closing price is in line with where the contract had been trading, or if there was a significant change in the final half an hour or so. If the latter, then the move can usually be disregarded (assuming no news came out towards the close). We need to heed the lessons from the Steven Bradbury Winter Olympic speed skating scenario; if we just look at the final result of the day's action (the closing price) we may miss something important. This is one reason why those who watch the markets all day actually gain some edge in doing so, as they have greater understanding of context than a trader who simply looks at the closing price.

I can still vividly remember the day when I first realised that equity closing prices could be manipulated; not only did I profit from this realisation at the time, the knowledge has also stayed with me ever since, and I still do not blindly trust closing prices. The stock in question was a small-cap Japanese stock called Toshoku, and I was a market-maker in the company's equity call warrant (a kind of call option). Toshoku was one of the most volatile stocks and warrants that were traded in our market, and it was a source of considerable losses both for my predecessor and for myself in my first few weeks of trading. It was not uncommon to lose $10 000 or $20 000 in one trading day just trading this warrant, as it jumped around so much — and bear in mind that as a market-maker I traded around one hundred and fifty different warrants.

This particular morning I saw that Toshoku stock had fallen by around 11 per cent, which was not an uncommon move. However, because I had a little more time than usual to price my warrants, I looked at the intra-day trading for Toshoku before setting my opening price. I saw that for most of the day the stock was only down by around 2 per cent, and that most of the fall occurred towards the end of the day and on low volume. So I decided that I didn't like the closing price and I made what was a very brave decision to mark my Toshoku warrant price only slightly lower than the previous day's close.

Initially when I did my pre-market price checks with other market-makers I was told that my price was too high, and both the traders that I spoke to sold me the maximum amount possible on my bid (I did lower my price after the first occasion, but was sold more even at the new lower price). I even had to stop conducting the pre-market price checks with other traders, as I normally would, because I was already at my limit for the Toshoku warrant. As the market was about to open I was extremely nervous; if I was wrong about the closing price I would stand to lose tens of thousands of dollars just on this one warrant.

When the market opened all the phone lines from the other market-makers immediately flashed, signalling that they were all calling in. The traders and assistants picked up the lines one by one, and every trader was asking for my price in Toshoku — clearly something was going on. My own assistant had rung another market-maker and told me that the price had now jumped by over four points since the pre-market checks. A US bank had gone around the market and bought up thousands of warrants at the lower levels and taken all the other market-makers short. It was clear that they had manipulated the share price down in order to get the warrant market-makers to call the price of the warrants lower.

My suspicion about the closing price was justified and I made over $20 000 profit in the first few minutes of trading just on the Toshoku warrant. I cannot describe how good it felt to have finally worked out what was happening and then to profit from that new knowledge. It was the first time that I had ever made a significant profit on that warrant, and I had learned a lesson that has stayed with me and served me well since: do not always trust closing prices.

Constructing watchlists

Having explained the reasons why we need to construct watchlists in a certain manner, and what we're trying to do with them, I will now explain how to actually construct them. I use two types of watchlists: a macro watchlist, and then micro watchlists. I'll start by looking at macro watchlists.

Macro watchlists

As the name suggests, macro watchlists are our source of information about what is happening in world markets. Our global macro watchlist is our first source of information each day. I suggest grouping markets by asset type rather than country. So, for example, we will include the major global share indices, grouped together so that we can see how various share markets have performed. Then we will do likewise with bonds while also adding major currency cross rates and major commodities. Doing this means we have fulfilled our goal of including positively and inversely correlated markets and we will be analysing the actions of a very wide range of participants from around the globe.

Depending on which broking firm you use you may be able to construct watchlists on one of the platforms that they provide. This is one area where CFD firms are good in that their platforms typically cover all markets. While we may not choose to trade on their platforms, they can provide an easy way to construct and monitor watchlists.

For those who are more computer literate, you can also construct a watchlist within a spreadsheet taking the data required either from a broker platform or from sources on the internet. Some of my clients have done this and they have created some excellent watchlists with the bonus of being able to construct the watchlist in the way that suits them. We all have different preferences for the way in which we like to visualise information, so if you can construct your own watchlist you will be able to design one that you can relate to more easily.

Table 5.1 shows some of the main components of a global macro watchlist grouped together by asset. Other markets can be added but this is the minimum required. With regards to commodities we can include spot prices, futures prices or both; it is up to you. If you plan to trade a commodity product as your specialisation then you could include all these forms in your micro watchlist (discussed in the next section). A look through this type of watchlist each morning will quickly inform you of what is happening across a range of different markets and you will learn how markets move and spot which moves may be out of step. Any large or strange move should then be investigated further. For example if you are used to seeing an inverse relationship between the US Dollar and Gold and on one day they both rally sharply then this would need further investigation. Remember that correlations are not set in stone but when they change they are telling us that something interesting is occurring.

For most private traders other pieces of information, such as credit default swap prices, are unlikely to be found on your broker platform, so these will need to be looked up on the internet. Saving these to your browser's favourites means this only adds a matter of a few minutes each day, but if you construct your own watchlist on a spreadsheet then these can be included there.

Table 5.1: main components of a global macro watchlist

Bonds	Stocks	Currencies	Commodities
US	DIJA	EUR/USD	Gold
UK	S&P 500	USD/YEN	Silver
GER	NASDAQ	EUR/YEN	Crude oil (WTI)
Japan	FTSE	GBP/USD	Crude oil (Brent)
Italy	DAX	USD/CHF	Copper
	MIB	AUD/USD	
	NIKKEI		
	Hang Seng		

We then seek out any market news that may have come out—'news' being specific events or data, including bond auctions, for example, or interest rate decisions. We are not looking for opinions on markets; we are only seeking actual events. It's our job to then determine what the effect of the event was on the market and/or the effect that the event may have had on our trades.

So, really, global macro watchlists are quite straightforward and generally only take up around 15 minutes of our time each day (for someone experienced in looking at them; it may take you longer to start with). On many days, there is little movement and so not much more to investigate. Other times we might need to research some more—for example, if we see some movement in bonds, we would want to check out the whole yield curve to check whether the curve has changed. All large moves should be investigated.

Micro watchlists

As specialists we will be trading one specific market, or perhaps a sector if you're a share trader. So, having gained an understanding of what has happened to world markets from our macro watchlist, our next task is to conduct a more detailed investigation of our chosen specialist contract or sector. Again, when we are constructing these micro watchlists we should include both positively and inversely correlated markets and draw from a variety of markets to get views from as many participants as possible. However, we are only interested in markets that have a close relationship with our own, so some markets will be left out (but they'll be on our global watchlist).

As an example I'll run through the process of setting up a micro watchlist for a trader who trades gold futures or perhaps gold shares (they will have similar watchlists).

Obviously they will start with gold futures and also, if possible, the spot gold price. Then they'll add silver futures and platinum too — the other precious metals. This helps to weigh up whether any move in their gold contract is restricted to gold or has occurred across all precious metals.

Then they will add other commodities such as copper futures, and perhaps oil futures too. This is to reference whether any move in precious metals has been replicated among other commodities. They would want to see whether precious metals are acting differently from other commodities, as this can provide useful information and context.

Next our gold trader will add either the US Dollar Index or some US dollar cross rates, or both. This is to see whether any move in gold (and other commodities) is related to movement in the US dollar. As gold is priced in US dollars, there can often be an inverse relationship in their respective prices (US dollar up, gold down). They'd need to check if this has occurred or if any recent correlation has changed.

Finally they should add some gold shares from around the world. These are a different set of participants again, and so our trader should check what they have been up to. Obviously for traders who are trading gold stocks, this last group is an important one to take cues from.

Any significant moves or changes to recent correlations in any of these markets or contracts should be investigated further. For stocks there might be some corporate news to digest.

So our gold micro watchlist contains a number of different markets that are all linked to gold. If, for example, we see that the gold price has risen we do not simply take this as being bullish; we want to understand the context of the move. We can quickly see if other precious metals and/or other commodities have rallied, and we can check if the move may have been currency related. If there is an element of panic in markets, and perhaps gold was responding to that, we would have picked this up from our macro watchlist and our review of products such as credit default swaps. So we still have other avenues covered. Any trade or decision we make is backed by a range of information and an understanding of the context of the trade.

Again, the time taken on a micro watchlist may only be around 15 to 30 minutes per day—nothing excessive. The hard work has been done prior to setting up the watchlists, in terms of building up our knowledge. Once this vital foundation has been laid, we can save time. Typically professional traders will spend around an hour or so analysing overnight activity through watchlists and news (if needed) prior to making their decisions. This is all done before the markets open to ensure that we are ready to act as soon as possible.

So, armed with the knowledge of how to compile watchlists, and now with an example as well as a rundown on constructing one, I hope that you will be able to construct your own. Remember that some information may not be available on the watchlists; use of the internet may be required too. In terms of sources for further information such as news, it's important to use a trusted firm such as Bloomberg. Most brokers offer news feeds and there are some good websites too, including the Bloomberg website.

Other information to be gathered

There is some other research that we need to conduct in addition to the watchlists. Every morning we need to check which data (economic, company, and so on) is due out so that we can plan for it and include this in our decision making. It's a good idea every Monday to see what is coming up for the current week so that we can plan in advance—it's always better to be planning one or two days ahead of the market.

It's often stated that there is a battle between fundamental analysis and technical analysis. The former is usually stated to be analysis of company balance sheets and detailed economic forecasting, and I think that I've explained enough about technical analysis. To me this is a false battle, as from what I have seen both sides are unreliable. I would like to offer an alternative view of the analysis that we should employ that I will term the 'traders' fundamentals'. For traders who are short-term operators, our analysis needs to include anything that can affect the demand and supply, and therefore the price, of the contract that we trade. That is why we include data, earnings, and so on; because clearly these will affect the price, while the stock borrow situation can also affect the demand and supply. The same can also be true of margin changes for products such as futures. Increases to margin rates for futures will often lead to losing positions, in particular having to exit. These sorts of issues cannot be simply ignored and they also form part of our regular analysis and research.

If your product has derivatives listed on it (for example, exchange-traded futures, which usually have options as a derivative) then it's worthwhile investigating those derivatives on at least a weekly basis. Finding out whether there have been any significant derivative trades or changes to open interest can provide useful information that, again, many participants ignore. For example, large quantities of put buying on your product could indicate that some traders have become bearish or are at least hedging for a downside move. Once again we find that knowledge, in this case of derivatives, can provide extra insight and add to our understanding of the markets and current context.

Previously, when I traded markets that had a large number of technical traders, such as futures markets, I used to look over any technical levels (support and resistance, and so on) and chart patterns, trendlines, and so on, to see if the market I was trading was close to any of significance. This, of course, wasn't because I wanted to jump on these technical trades; rather, I wanted to be aware of what those traders might be doing and where they might be active. For equity markets, where I think technical traders are in a small minority, I wasn't so interested in these technical levels. In recent times I have become less concerned with these technical traders and so I no longer regularly check their patterns, levels and indicators. Algorithmic and high-frequency traders probably have more impact on our markets nowadays but, as they are all doing different things, we are usually unable to work out where they will trade.

Using the watchlists to trade

Watchlists are our primary source of information; they provide us with objective information on the markets. We must then gather the information and assess what it's telling us and then decide which way we need to be positioned in our specialist contract. It's important to state that the watchlist is not our only source of analysis for trading, even though it is our primary source of data. That is because we have to weigh up other issues, such as what is being priced into the contract (discussed in more depth in chapter 8).

The following are generalisations and simplifications of using watchlists to trade, and are methods of trading that are basically momentum-based. I use them purely as examples of how we use watchlist information if it's being used in conjunction with our other analysis.

Generally, if all information is pointing in the same direction then we may instigate a trade of our chosen contract in that same direction. We will hold the position but continue to monitor the watchlists and exit the trade if and when the information changes, and/or if we are stopped out of the position. Of course, while we hold the trade we are always looking for disconfirming information, which will usually come from markets other than our own. If there is data due to come out then we also need to weigh up what's being priced in to our contract, which may change our choice of trade. Any trading decision made on data alone, without weighing up what is being priced in, is likely to be less robust.

There are many occasions, though, when not all the information agrees—so what should we do? If most information points one way and only, say, one market suggests otherwise, then we still might want to enter the trade—but we can reduce our position size to reflect the small amount of contrary evidence. We can also decide to do nothing, which is the safer option.

Having written that disconfirmation is what we use to exit a trade, I can understand if you think it odd that I would still suggest to trade when there is disconfirmation. That is one alternative; there is always the possibility of doing nothing, and this reflects the fact that each of us is different, with different tolerances for risk. The reality is that there are many instances when not all information lines up, and sometimes it may only be a small piece of disconfirming data. I recognise that some traders may still want to trade. By understanding the context, though, they will be able to be on alert and be aware of the extra risk they are taking.

Note that if we decide to trade I have advocated a reduction in the trading size to reflect the higher degree of risk. This is a reflection of proactive position sizing, which I espouse and will explain in chapter 7. With this kind of trade, as we are already aware of some disconfirmation, we will also be on heightened alert for further evidence. If the one disconfirming market changes to agree with the others, then the trader with the smaller position can look to increase to her normal size, while a trader who sat out can now enter the trade. At the first sign of other markets moving towards the contrary, we will immediately exit the trade and remain vigilant for the opportunity to enter the opposite trade. If there is a complete difference of opinion between various markets, then, while this is interesting, we will not trade until we have a significant majority in one direction.

I must reiterate that analysis of what is being priced in and data releases must be considered too. Trading is not an 'X + Y = trade' type of scenario; there is a range of factors to weigh up in our decision making.

Think laterally

Building knowledge of a variety of markets and learning how they fit together offers us a further advantage: the opportunity to think laterally. By this I mean the ability to look at what is happening in one market and then being able to see how that might affect other markets. Traders who can think laterally and act appropriately will find themselves ahead of others, sometimes significantly. The ability to think laterally will greatly increase the number of trading opportunities that you will find.

I'll use an example from my own career. I was trading for a large European bank and it was mid 2001. Stocks all over the world were weak, with technology shares faring particularly badly as the bubble was bursting. The head of equities had asked all senior traders to come up with ideas to hedge the equity department's broking division, as the firm was rightly concerned that falling stock markets would lead to lower volumes and therefore lower profits for the broking arm.

The standard hedge for equities would be to buy put options, either on individual shares or on indices. (Put options increase in value as the contract falls.) However, due to the already steep declines in share markets, the price of put options was very high and they offered a poor risk-to-reward for the hedge that we wanted; in particular, we would have had to outlay a considerable amount of money for what was only supposed to be a hedge trade. After a few days we were still no closer to finding a good trade.

Then, thinking laterally, I looked at the price of interest rate call options; these would increase in value if interest rates fell. My reasoning was that if shares continued to fall sharply and volatility increased, central banks (in particular the US Federal Reserve) would step in and lower rates, as they had done at other times of instability. What I discovered was that interest rate call options were not pricing in such rate cuts, and so the call options that I wanted offered very good value. We bought some of these options and they made a significant profit when, very soon after, the US Federal Reserve did indeed start to cut rates.

This trade was driven by knowledge of different markets and products, and I cannot stress enough how crucial knowledge is to success. There are no short cuts; a long-term sustainable trading career can only be built on a solid foundation of knowledge. Knowledge will provide opportunities and help us to think independently and outside the box, where the real trading edge often lies.

Watchlists and our core principles

Let's relate our watchlists to our core principles. The ability to preserve our capital, essential if we are to enjoy a long-term career, requires the ability to spot potential risk. Biases such as confirmation bias will be a hindrance in this regard, as will relying on noise and subjective views. Good watchlists help to eliminate these obstacles, helping us to spot potential danger and to proactively manage our risk.

The watchlists will play a significant role in helping us to understand context and engage our System 2 mindset. If we consult our watchlist every day we will build an excellent idea of the context of the markets we are trading. We should become aware when market conditions are changing, and our decision making will be enhanced. Eliminating context is a short cut that many private traders use, and it weakens their decision making.

By studying many markets and their various interactions and correlations, we are undoubtedly having to employ a slower, more thoughtful mindset. There are no short cuts in our decision making, and any significant moves will receive even further investigation. As we become more proficient at reading watchlists we will become quicker at analysing them, but this does not mean that we are abandoning our System 2—it just means that some actions are moving to the part of the brain that deals with actions that have become like second nature.

Summary

- Understand the difference between information and noise.
- Track a range of different markets that correlate and interact in different ways.
- Build up a picture of the current market context.
- Always look for disconfirming or new information.

Chapter 6

It's a business;
treat it that way

In this chapter...

We investigate the business-type decisions that traders face. Treating trading as a business means that you as the trader are the boss, with all the responsibility associated with that position. While many employees believe that they can do a better job than their boss, the reality is that many if not most would actually struggle with the range of decisions that a business owner has to make. Whether you want to trade for a living or you view trading as a challenge and are trying to generate extra income, you must view trading as a business.

The failure rate among many businesses is high, and that's the case for trading too. By specialising we are already employing one of the key traits of successful businesses: specialists can learn their market inside and out and are more likely to spot subtle changes to market conditions. Most successful business operators specialise in what they know best and over time they gather experience of their market that also provides edge over new entrants; traders should also act in this business-minded way.

In addition to the trading-related analysis and decisions that we face, we also need to weigh up other aspects of running a business, such as the costs involved and deciding which broker and platforms to use. This is another area that will require a good deal of due diligence before you trade. If you choose the wrong type of broker, pay commissions that are too high or use an unreliable trading platform, then your trading will suffer.

Which broker?

This is the arguably the most important decision that we make in this regard: which broker to use. Rather than recommend any specific broker, I will instead explain what to look for in a broker.

Some brokers (sometimes referred to as 'clearers' for futures) have specific arrangements for active, more professional-style traders, while others concentrate more on the 'mum and dad' amateur-style traders. Obviously we need to seek the former. For contracts such as futures and shares, the better brokers will offer a range of trading platforms from a variety of providers. This will allow us to choose the platform of our choice. If you want to trade these products and are only offered a proprietary platform to trade on or are offered just one rebadged platform, then it's likely that the broker is not for you. For FX markets the situation can be different, as it's more usual for each broker to offer their own proprietary platform—but again, if possible, look for a firm that offers more than one. The more platforms on offer the more chance we have of using one that is better than other traders use and that keeps pace with technological changes. If you have to use your broker's own platform and they don't keep pace with technological advances, then you could well be disadvantaged.

When brokers offer only their own proprietary platform, it's often because you can only trade on their prices; these are called market-maker platforms. They are common for CFDs and also for FX providers. For futures, commodities and shares I strongly suggest against using one of these platforms. You will effectively be trading against the 'house' trader, on a price that's not transparent enough for our purposes. Further, you will usually be a price-taker—that is, unable to buy on the bid side or even work an order in the middle of the spread. I write in chapter 1 how important the spread is; the best traders want to set the spread and trade inside it if possible. If we always have to trade on the 'wrong' side of the spread, then we'll be giving away a lot of money each year. The more we trade, the more we give away if we can't trade on the spread as the real professionals do.

For active traders who trade many times per week or per month, every cent on every trade adds up. Trading on the 'amateur' side of the spread can cost thousands of dollars per year. For example, a futures trader who trades ten lots per week and always gives away a spread of even just one tick of $10 will be effectively losing $100 per week, or $5200 per year. If you trade a futures-type contract on a CFD platform, then typically you'll have to take the spread and lose that money (to the market-maker). However, if you trade directly into the real futures market on the exchange, then you can trade on better terms and potentially save that $5200. Indeed, often the CFD 'futures' equivalents have wider spreads than the 'real' exchange versions, but they are marketed as 'commission free'. For active traders it usually works out better to pay commissions and trade a tighter spread.

For FX traders the situation is a little different because so many of the platforms force you to take the spread. If you find a platform that allows you to set the price and trade inside the spread, that's great. If not, there is little you can do except to be aware that very short-term trading (scalping) is significantly harder under these circumstances. Your trades will likely have to be held for longer because of the edge (the spread) that you are paying away.

I have a strong preference for trading exchange-traded products; they are more transparent, we can clearly see the order book, we can switch from one broker to another without changing the prices that we can trade, we can trade inside the spread or set the spread and, vitally, we can trade directly against those who we have edge over.

Those who wish to trade shares have a problem in that CFDs offer the easiest way to trade using leverage and also to short sell—but usually CFDs are market-maker platforms. For short-term traders, these do not offer all the advantages that we need. If you do choose to trade shares using CFDs I would suggest you conduct significant research into your choice of broker.

Liquidity

Market-maker platforms also throw up another problem: the issue of liquidity. When you trade an over-the-counter product such as a market-maker CFD or broker FX rate, it's essentially only a deal between you and the provider. You must take their price only, and the trade can't be switched over to another broker or provider. You are trading against and only with the broker. Traditional share traders can usually have their positions switched to another broker and also will trade on the price at the exchange. Similarly, futures traders are trading a product that is backed by the exchange and against prices and orders that come from multiple participants. Further, there have been examples when futures positions have been taken over by another broker or clearer, and this can only occur because the broker is not taking the other side to the trade. Where the broker is taking the other side to your trade, only they can get you out of it, a situation that I believe is not ideal for us.

In fact many (if not most) hedge funds and investment bank traders are not allowed to trade an instrument where only one firm makes the price and offers liquidity. This situation is rightly regarded as unsatisfactory for liquidity purposes — traders are too reliant on one person or firm to exit a trade. Liquidity is a risk that we need to consider and mitigate, and it's a risk that too many private traders fail to consider.

Commissions

Ideally we want a broker who acknowledges and rewards us as active traders, preferably by offering a sliding scale of commissions that decreases the more we trade. Again, if you are trading a 'commission-free' market-maker or broker platform, this cannot occur — but, of course, these platforms aren't really commission-free; you're usually paying more in terms of a higher spread, and this does not change whether you trade once a year or once a minute. Again, good brokers understand and have products and allowances for active traders; these are the firms we should look to use.

The more we trade, the more commissions become an issue for us. Also, if we make short-term trades for small edge, low commissions will be essential if we are to be profitable. As with any business, those with the lowest cost base will have edge over their competitors and will find it easier to find winning trades and a profitable career. Therefore, low commissions and/or a very low bid/offer spread (or the ability to set the spread) are essential to us. The ideal scenario for active, short-term traders is low commissions and the ability to trade at the price of our choice; there are a number of futures clearing or broking firms that offer this.

Safety

The safety of our funds has been a hot topic for the past few years after some notable broker collapses. First, it's important that the broker we use separates clients' funds from their own. It used to be thought that the larger the firm the better—as larger firms were less likely to fail. However, the collapse of some major firms, including MF Global, has shown that belief to be invalid. I still think it's preferable to use a firm with a good history, and that offers the other advantages that I discuss in this section. We can further protect ourselves by leaving only the funds we need to trade in our account and taking out our profits regularly. These profits can be our income, but also reserve funds (for reasons that I explain later in this chapter). Brokers will not like me for suggesting that you should continually transfer your funds out of the trading account, because they can make significant amounts on these client funds due to the fact they pay little or no interest. This is another example of how the industry professionals make their money by taking small amounts but doing so regularly. The ability to easily access our funds and transfer them to and from our trading account is also a necessity.

Good customer support is essential, too, in particular the ability to have trades executed by the broking firm in the event that your internet connection goes down. For this reason a firm with a

24-hour desk is preferable so that we have support whenever we might need it.

We require brokers who offer us the tools (news feeds and so on) that we want. I encourage you to ask as many questions as you can of potential brokers; good ones will always be happy to answer and will respond in a professional and courteous manner. Those who have many professional trader clients will understand exactly what you need and will also understand that we are searching for edge through low commissions and a good platform.

What to pay for

Traders today are bombarded with advertisements proclaiming the benefits of a wide range of products: trading platforms, backtesting software, charting software, products to help track our positions, newsletters and news wires—these are just a sample of the types of products on offer. It's possible for traders to spend thousands of dollars a month on these products, but we need to make sure that we're only paying for products that add value.

As with any business, profitability is revenue minus costs—so we need to examine our costs closely while ensuring that we have systems and products that allow us to achieve our goals and, if possible, provide us with edge over other participants.

I have always found it amusing that one of the most popular questions that I'm asked is 'How many screens do you have?' I've found that many retail traders seem to believe that professional traders have lots of screens, and the more screens the better. So I can now categorically state that there is no direct link between the number of screens we use and our success. We are not trying to impress anyone with the suite of products that we use; we're trying to maximise our profitability.

Computers

We need to start with the primary tool of our business, which is our computer. We require a very good quality computer with fast processing capacity and a good graphics capability. I also suggest that the computer that you trade on should be used only for trading so it's not clogged up with other programs and applications that might slow it down.

Trading platforms

The next most important tool for us is the trading platform, and the more often you trade, the more important a good trading platform is. As I wrote previously, good brokers offer a range of platforms and they can usually be trialled for free. It's rare for a broker's proprietary platform to perform at the same level as a specialist trading platform. Particularly if you plan to trade futures, it's worth using a good platform with a fast and reliable data feed. For day traders in particular, a good trading platform provides edge over other participants and it is edge that we should be happy to pay for.

Internet

To compete with other traders from around the world requires a reliable and fast internet connection. Again, it's worth paying extra for a dedicated fast line—and always choose the fastest speed you can get. If you're an active trader or day trader you require a fast internet speed to gain edge. If your speeds are significantly slower than others then they will have edge over you. I can speak from experience here following my move to a small town in regional Western Australia. I had underestimated the effect of a poor internet speed and found that I was missing trades that I used to get. Further, the internet connection here can be very unreliable and, all too often, can be down for substantial periods of time. Make sure that your internet provider is reliable, as some of the cheaper providers can offer a poor service with variable speeds.

News feeds

A trusted, reliable and live news feed is also required, particularly for intra-day traders who may need to respond to news and data releases. Fortunately most brokers offer third-party feeds from the major news wires. We also want the ability to have this feed displayed across our screen in a reduced-size window — that is, we want some flexibility with the feed to incorporate it into or around our trading platform so that we can easily and quickly see news headlines.

Charting packages

You will not be surprised to learn that this is not an essential for us. Most brokers and platforms provide a charting facility and, even if they're basic, they will be sufficient for our purposes. I prefer a trading platform that does not even have a charting facility, which has the added bonus of being cheaper. Now, having taught a number of private traders on the system without charts, most of them, too, see the benefit of not having them. This is certainly an area where further expense can be ruled out. Many private traders pay for fancy charting systems that simply do not provide edge. In addition, many brokers offer fancy charting packages to tempt traders to use them rather than offer cheaper commissions or better spreads; this is a common feature of CFD and FX platforms. However, cheaper commissions, tighter spreads and the ability to make the price *actually do* provide edge — whereas fancy charts do not. Charts are no substitute for real edge.

It's actually quite common for broking firms to offer all kinds of tools that offer no edge, such as charting systems and analysts' research. This is all part of the financial junk-food industry and, while they appeal to 'mum and dad' and other amateur traders, professionals are not enticed by these items of trading bling. So, as independent-minded traders who want to make objective decisions about our trades, we should not be enticed into paying for broker research reports or other tip sheets or newsletters.

If you think that trading requires fancy charting packages and lots of technical devices, think back to the futures pit traders. They were armed only with a pencil and trading cards and their brains when they took on all comers in the pits. What they did pay for was the privilege to stand in the pit and be able to set the prices and trade on the 'professional' side of the spread. They got huge edge from doing so, hence the success rate among floor traders was higher than the norm for the futures industry.

Interestingly, when the futures markets went screen-based, the early trading platforms did not offer them the opportunity to act in the same way. So many ended up buying chart packages and other analysis tools and they ended up trading like those they had previously profited from. Many did not survive to see the day when trading platforms improved and market-making skills could be employed again.

What capital is required?

The age-old question: How much capital do I need? There really is no one definitive answer, as it depends on the style of trading you choose. As I will demonstrate later in the book, it's possible to make a decent living using a relatively small amount of capital. However, that style of trading (scalping) will not appeal to all. Traders will usually need to use leverage in order to achieve better returns. This means that we will need to be very disciplined and to cut losses quickly — otherwise leverage can get you into trouble.

I have a strong preference for trading styles that result in many trades of small profits that are compounded to produce an overall good return. These usually require smaller trading capital, too. Too many retail traders throw large sums of money around on each trade in the false belief that making good returns requires larger trading sizes. They take too many risks in the quest to hit trading home runs.

As with any business, insufficient capital can lead to failure. However, for private traders this is probably more of an issue with trading style than capital. You should choose a trading style around the capital that you have, rather than choose a trading style and then realise you have no funds left after a few large losses.

As I wrote earlier, we only need sufficient trading capital in our account for the trading that we are conducting. Any funds in excess of that should be transferred out of the broker account and into an interest-bearing account at another institution (broker accounts typically pay little or no interest). It may not be the case that we are always looking to grow our trading size and therefore our trading capital.

The decision of whether to grow or not is one faced by many business operators, and the answer is not always simple. To begin with, you almost certainly will not be trading in the size or manner to which you aspire. We will all look to grow and increase our trading size from where we first start, but of course this requires us to be successful; we must not grow our size unless or until we are making consistent profits. Depending on your trading style and the contract you trade, it might not be possible to increase too much. For example, going back to the very early days of futures screen trading, I was scalping (very fast day trading, which I will explain in chapter 10) FTSE futures. I started trading single lots at a time, then increased to two contracts — but when I tried to go to three my performance did not improve, because sometimes the depth was not there. I was making decent profits with two contracts at a time, so I happily went back to two. If I wanted to trade in larger sizes I would have had to trade a different contract.

There can come a time when we are happy with what we are making relative to the capital we are risking, in which case there is no need to continue to grow our trading account. I have known some traders who want to try to become big traders in their market, but this mostly ends in trouble. Markets have a habit of taking from those who are greedy, as greed is often accompanied by excessive risk. We need to know our limits and the limits of our risk tolerance; if you get to a position where you are happy with your trading and profitability then that's great — it's where we want to be. The point that I would like to make here is that trading is not simply about trying to become a multimillionaire (despite what the financial junk-food industry tells you). There is nothing wrong with earning a good income doing a job you love where you are your own boss and enjoy winning the many challenges that you face.

Time required

I regularly attend the monthly meetings of my local chamber of commerce (a business group). Imagine the reaction there if I suggested to the local small business operators that business success can be achieved by working just a couple of hours a week. I doubt anyone of them would take me seriously. So why do so many private traders believe that they can achieve sustainable success even if they put in limited time? Obviously the junk-food industry plays its part, but retail traders also need to take responsibility for their actions.

Investment bank and hedge-fund traders often spend 12 hours or more a day at their desks, weighing up trades and analysing their positions. If they could achieve similar results in less time, I'm sure they would all gladly do so. Bear in mind, too, that they have many people helping them, such as assistants and risk managers. I do not expect private traders to have the time or desire to spend the same amount of time as bank traders but, as with most things in life, the more you put in the more you can get out. While the watchlists that I have described will help you to use your time well, with the various risks and outcomes that we need to weigh up, trading should still take up at least an hour or two on most days. The more you watch the markets the more in tune with them you can become and the better you will understand context, because you will witness it in action. It's easier to understand context when you are watching or, better still, participating in real time, as opposed to looking back at a graph or data after the market has closed.

It's essential to make the most of the time we have, so we must dedicate our analysis to information and not noise—hence the importance of chapter 5. By cutting out noise such as rumours, tips, and the huge variety of opinions that are out there, we can save significant time as well as remaining focused on real information.

It's possible that many private traders do have the time to dedicate to trading, it's just that they're using their time poorly. In terms of analysis our time needs to be spent watching the markets, weighing up what is being priced in and the effect of possible future outcomes. This is difficult enough without adding noise into the mix. In the same way that we should only pay for products that provide edge, we should spend most or all of our time on efforts that provide edge; these include our knowledge of markets and products.

If you're trading alongside a full-time job I understand that it can be hard to find the time, but you should try to find an hour or two either before you go to work or after work. In addition, the weekend can be a good time to catch up with some more detailed analysis. If you simply do not have the time to give to trading, then you need to reconsider whether to trade. The dream of sitting by a pool spending half an hour a day on trading and making lots of money is a furphy spread by the financial junk-food industry to entice new participants. All of the better traders that I have known and worked with work very hard for their success and would get angry at the suggestion that success can be achieved with minimal effort. Remember, the short cuts that we are told will help to save time, such as technical analysis indicators, chart patterns, and so on, are unreliable; they're short cuts to failure for most who use them.

Practise properly

Before we trade for real money in any new market, product or technique we will need to practise and trial our strategies and analysis to make sure they work. Most platforms offer demonstration modes nowadays where we can trade into live markets using a demonstration account—these are ideal. One key point to remember about practising, though, is that you must practise in exactly the same manner as you expect to trade. Following on from that, you must take your results as they are.

I have seen on too many occasions traders make comments such as 'With real money I would have cut that trade earlier so the trade wouldn't have been that bad' or ' I wouldn't have done that trade with a live account; I was just giving it a go because it's not real money'. It's quite simply a poor effort to practise in this way; not only are you showing a capacity for lack of discipline, but your practise results cannot be taken seriously as a reflection of what you might achieve.

I have for some years now coached junior soccer players, and one of the continuing struggles with young players is their tendency to try and mess around during training. They love the game and are usually switched on for it, but many view training as a necessary chore; they only come because they won't get selected for the game if they don't. Every year I need to instil into them the idea that you play as you practise — if you practise poorly then you will play poorly. If you watch a professional golfer on the practise range you will see the same philosophy; they concentrate on every shot. Even if they are practising something simple such as a three-foot putt, they will aim for 100 per cent accuracy.

I believe that the way we practise actually reflects the person we are and offers a sign of how we will fare as traders. Bearing in mind that discipline is such an important part of trading, if you lack discipline with your demonstration trades then you are likely to struggle with real money trading. Do not switch from a demonstration account to a real account unless or until you are consistently trading profitably and are demonstrating exactly the skills and discipline that you want to see replicated with real money. It is your money that you will lose if you fail in this regard.

Plan B

Being business-minded means that we need to have plans for when things go wrong, in particular with systems, internet, and so on. We need to have back-up plans for as many eventualities as possible. These events are rare, but I can say from experience that they do occur, so it's worth having plans in place.

Losing internet connection can be a significant problem, especially for active day traders and particularly if we have an open position. This is where having phone access to a 24-hour broking desk is required, as it provides the ability to exit trades. If your broker is based overseas, make sure that there is an easy access number for international callers. As I discussed earlier, this is part of our broker due diligence.

Computer failure is rare, but obviously has the ability to stop us from being able to trade. I explained earlier that we should use a computer that is dedicated to trading, but as a backup it's worth downloading your trading platform to another computer for use in case of emergency. Remember too to download updates, when they occur, to the backup computer.

Broker failure or collapse is another issue that we need to think about. In this regard we can try to cover ourselves in two ways. First, by only keeping the minimum amount required in our trading accounts and transferring funds back to our own interest-bearing accounts, we can both protect ourselves from losing too much if the worst happens and also look to build up additional trading capital that we can then use to trade through another broker. Also, if we trade exchange-traded products we have the possibility of transferring our trades to another broker. (Please note this is a possibility, not a certainty, but it's worth considering). As explained previously, trading an over-the-counter product will often mean that if the broker collapses your trades will be lost.

As is often the case in business, there can be times when it's more difficult to make money without taking undue risk even for professional traders. Typically these can be times of low volatility, low volumes and/or sideways movement. The fact is that trading is not a salaried business — even for the best traders some years will be better than others. By developing the skills to trade in as many different conditions as possible, for example by using derivatives, we can reduce the number of times when we cannot trade — but during a trading career we will undoubtedly encounter some tough years. During these times it's essential that we remain disciplined and don't chase profits by any means, as such actions can lead to losses and the adverse psychological effects of doing something you knew was wrong.

We should also remember one of the core rules, preservation of capital, is still in play. It's important to stay in the business because we can only take advantage of future good trading times if we keep our capital. For good traders there can be rewards over the long term, but we need to make it there, which is why we need to survive the short term — this is the importance of capital preservation.

As with any business we can look to cut some costs if possible during quiet times — but we shouldn't have much by way of excess costs anyway if we're managing our business properly. The funds that we set aside for possible broker failure can also be seen as a general buffer fund that can be used if required in these times. As with life in general, it's always prudent to set aside funds during good times for when times are not so good.

While knowledgeable traders can find good trades in more market conditions than those with less knowledge, it would be wrong of me to suggest that there are good profits to be had all of the time. It's important that you approach this business with realistic expectations (hence the need for this section).

As for trades themselves, the next chapter will cover position management—but for now the key discipline is to cut losses quickly. Small losses will not wipe you out but large losses will. So our Plan B for when a trade goes against us is to simply to cut it and take the loss. Remember the broker from chapter 2 who bought shares only to see them fall quite substantially and yet he held them. When I asked him if he used stop loss levels he replied that he didn't; he only bought good companies and would simply keep the position. He had no Plan B due to his overconfidence (some might call it arrogance).

As with everything in life, it's great when everything goes well but we need to plan for when things don't go so well. There are many different ways to incur losses as a trader, and these include platform failure and computer crashes. As the old saying goes, 'if you fail to prepare, be prepared to fail'.

Tax advice

Every jurisdiction has its own tax rates and policies and we need to either keep pace with these or, preferably, seek expert advice. To start with, we need to know how to structure our business for tax and company purposes. This should obviously be done before you start trading. The right advice here can save tens of thousands of dollars over a career. Moving on, we will need good advice on issues such as what services and systems we can claim back. Some countries have specialist tax rules for traders, others do not. If possible, seek assistance from an adviser who understands trading and has helped other traders. As in any business, surrounding ourselves with good advisers can be extremely beneficial.

Re-evaluate

I have explained how, with our trading, we need to regularly look out for new information and change our thinking if required. The same is true for the topics covered in this chapter. While this is an ongoing activity, I would suggest a scheduled re-evaluation at least every six months.

The re-evaluation will investigate if our broker is still offering us the same services and hopefully improving them. We need to check this because firms have been known to reduce the phone broking services and/or change commission rates. Be alert for new broking firms or new products and services being offered by other firms. If you see something new, the first thing to do is to contact your current broker and see if they have plans to introduce the new service too. It's preferable to develop a good relationship with a broker and to move only if we have to, but if any changes occur that mean your trading can be advantaged by moving or disadvantaged by staying, then this is something to be considered. As with the suggestions earlier in the chapter, make sure that any change of broker is backed by thorough due diligence — not just because of one new offering.

We need to keep abreast of advances in trading platforms so that we are always using the best we can afford. For active day traders good platforms provide significant edge over other traders, so this is an important area.

Examine your costs and ensure that everything you are paying for actually provides you with edge or vital information. For example, you might be paying for an exchange feed into your trading platform that you no longer look at; or perhaps you can change a price feed from real time to delayed because it's not a primary source of information for your trading.

This is all part of being business-minded and trying to be the best business operator that we can. In turn this will help our profitability, remembering that sustainable success will come from compounding as many profits as possible, and often from compounding seemingly small amounts. There is a saying: 'Look after the pennies and the pounds will look after themselves.'

Summary

- We need to be business-minded.
- Conduct thorough due diligence on brokers, trading platforms, and so on.
- Only pay for products that provide edge.
- Prepare and practice properly.
- Have back-up plans.
- Re-evaluate regularly.

Chapter 7

Position sizing and management

In this chapter ...

I explain my views about position sizing and position management, a complex topic that is often simplified too much by the financial junk-food industry.

Even as I set about planning this chapter I knew it would be the most difficult to write, so I need to set some expectations and parameters for what I will cover. It's not possible for me (or anyone) to write a simple step-by-step, how-to style trading book. The issues around position sizing and management can be complex, with a variety of scenarios, so trying to cover all bases and possibilities is virtually impossible in a book such as this; one could justify a whole book just on this topic. What I will do, though, is explain some core principles, which you will then need to incorporate into your trading. The principles that I espouse on this subject are grounded in the core rules that I set out at the start of part II, and also based on overcoming the psychological failings known to affect traders.

If there is one rule that I would urge over any other, it's to cut losses quickly. I learned this very early on in my career when I took over a highly volatile trading book of Japanese equity warrants. The timing of this was just a few months into what became the biggest stock market crash for over a generation. Graphs of the Nikkei during this period go nowhere near showing what it was like to trade during this time. Volatility was at times ridiculously high; sentiment to begin with was that the market was just correcting and would return to its previous bullishness. (Of course in hindsight everyone claims to have known that it was the bursting of a bubble, but I can assure you that at the time this was not the most widely held view.) Traders and investors were on an extraordinary roller-coaster that would deliver profits one day, then completely reverse to become a large loss the next.

The reason why I had the opportunity to trade at the age of 18 was because the existing traders at my firm were suffering significant losses. I was given what was regarded as the most volatile trading book, a book that the experienced traders did not want any involvement with. So, just six months after leaving high school, I was given a great opportunity — but one that came with a huge possibility of failure. To make matters worse for me, my promotion ahead of a number of other juniors meant that many on the desk would have been happy to see me fail; indeed, some actively tried to sabotage my trading. (That's a whole book in itself!)

Looking back, this was a great time to learn to trade because success during such a volatile time required both excellent analysis and discipline. The former required a degree of experience, and was something that I knew would take time to improve. However, discipline could be implemented immediately once I realised what needed to be done. When I looked at my own and the other traders' performances it was clear that sometimes only a few bad positions could wipe out profits from many more (we each traded around 150 warrants and typically kept positions in at least a third because, as market-makers, we had to allow other traders and fund managers to trade on our prices). Very quickly into my trading I made a simple decision that I have kept to for my whole trading career. I decided to cut losing positions quickly and adopted the philosophy of 'if I only hold winning trades I should only be able to make money'. The other traders on my desk believed that I cut trades too quickly—but day after day I would outperform them all. I relayed a second quote to them, one that I have subsequently used and heard many times since: 'The first cut is the cheapest.'

I do not want to face the difficulties of large losses that could possibly threaten my whole career. By cutting losses quickly I reduce that possibility significantly. To this day, many traders and particularly investors that I know believe that I cut losses too quickly, but I make no apologies for doing so; if I take care of losses, then profits usually take care of themselves. When I moved to trade with my own capital, I realised that preservation of my capital was my first goal and that cutting losses quickly would remain a fundamental discipline to employ.

In bull markets this kind of discipline can often be ignored, by private traders in particular, but I will stick to it nonetheless. It means that I am often much more conservative than other traders, but I'm comfortable with that. Bull markets always end—and when they do, if you have become accustomed to poor discipline, then it can be hard to change.

So let's examine some of the core philosophies of position sizing and management, remembering that these will need to be adapted to your own trading plan. Keep in mind that position sizing and position management are interrelated; they are not separate disciplines.

Position sizing

The first area to cover here is how much of our trading capital we should use per trade. The answer is not straightforward; it depends on whether we're using leverage or not. For those who don't use leverage (probably the minority of traders nowadays, and likely to be share traders), I would suggest using no more than 10 per cent of your trading capital in one trade. This allows you to enter a few trades, if required, while keeping some funds in reserve.

Most traders today use leverage in their trading through trading contracts such as futures, CFDs or FX, and so the idea of using

10 per cent of our trading capital per trade does not apply so well. It's crucially important that traders who use leverage don't overleverage, that they cut losses quickly and that they trade with a short-term time horizon. My suggestion is that the longer the time horizon for the trade, the less leverage we should use, predominantly due to the increased possibility of volatility.

Whether we use leverage or not, I strongly suggest that we should not risk more than 1 or 2 per cent of our trading capital per trade. That is, our stop loss level should be at a point that means that we should not lose more than 1 or 2 per cent of our overall capital.

For example, a trader with a $50 000 account who is not using leverage should allocate no more than $5000 per trade (10 per cent) and should have a stop loss that risks no more than 1 or 2 per cent of their account, in this case $500 to $1000. In reality, if he applies a stop loss level, as I explain later in this chapter, then usually he won't even be risking this much on the trade.

For a trader with a $50 000 account who is using leverage, it may well be that he takes a position in $30 000 in one trade; but he should still risk no more than $500 to $1000 on the trade.

However, please note that this is not how I set my stop loss—I'll explain that shortly—but when I do work out a stop loss level I must then refer it back to this rule and ensure that it meets the criteria. This is one of the areas of interaction between the various disciplines that we employ as part of position sizing and management.

As someone who favours proactive position sizing and management, I encourage a flexible approach to these disciplines. By that I mean that we don't always wait for the markets to move; we can try to proactively adjust our positions. I suggest using three different position sizes initially. One is used when we have full supporting evidence from our watchlists and other analysis (that is, everything points the same way and all analysis suggests we follow this momentum). The second is a smaller position size, perhaps half the size, and this is for the times when we have mostly supporting evidence but perhaps a little doubt. I explain this in chapter 6: by having this smaller position size we can choose to take the trade, but of course we can also choose to have no trade and wait for the situation to become clearer. Whichever you choose will depend on your personal risk tolerance. I also suggest a third, smaller position size to be used for speculative positions. These can be the macro-type trades that should not form part of our day-to-day trading because they are not backed by information; rather they reflect our views. I understand that all traders want speculative trades at times, but it's important that when we do so we use a smaller position size. Again, we can choose not to trade, but by employing a small position size we can reflect our view in a trade while risking only a small amount. The speculative size can also be used on the occasions when we believe the market may be too heavily positioned one way, perhaps ahead of some data. In these trades, we don't have evidence of a move but we know if one occurs it could be large and so the expected return of the trade may still be good. I will explain this type of trade further in chapter 8. I have often used option trades for these speculative, macro positions as they can be held for longer due to their smaller directional exposure to the market.

It's important to state that all trades, no matter what position size, should have stop loss levels in place, and none will be held to lose more than 1 to 2 per cent of our capital.

So these are examples of the flexible, proactive approach that I favour. It's one that is based on us having a good understanding of markets, as it requires the trader's judgement. However, keeping the maximum risk to 1 to 2 per cent means that we should always have a safety measure in place, which will be of great importance to inexperienced traders in particular. Undoubtedly we can all improve over time, and in the early stages of our trading career we need to be disciplined to stop us from losing our capital.

These types of methods will mean that we need to judge each situation differently; we don't simply employ the same size and strategy over and over again. I believe this is how trading should be, because each situation we face is likely to be different from the last. This does test our judgement, but that's what trading should be: a test of our skill and analysis. If we get it wrong we will lose, but at least by having a stop loss in place we can stop ourselves from losing too much. As I've said before, by taking on the challenge of trading we are trying to find out if we have the capacity and the skills to become successful. We need to find that out for ourselves, and trying to copy someone else's exact method or formula is unlikely to work; trading is not that kind of business.

Another situation that requires judgement of position sizing relates to volatility. Volatility is a concept that is sometimes misunderstood and often ignored by retail traders, and I cover it in more depth in part III. For the purposes of this chapter, what I want to explain is that if we are concerned about the possibility of rising volatility, or are in a higher volatility environment, then we should use one of the smaller position sizes. This is because volatility itself can lead to us being stopped out of a trade, so we may need to enter the trade more than once.

By reducing our trading size when we have less supporting evidence for a trade or when volatility is rising or high, we are reflecting the information that we see. It makes sense to me to reduce the position size according to conditions; to have a larger position when I have more information or if volatility is lower. Too many traders and, in my opinion, too many trading courses, employ the same position size for each trade and the only change occurs to increase or decrease the size as the overall account size changes. Investment bank and hedge-fund traders have risk management systems and product controllers to help with this type of decision making. So when volatility is higher, they may be forced to trade in smaller size. Private traders don't have this support, so I'm trying to replicate the effect—although it's the trader's responsibility to assess and act. When we trade for ourselves we must also adopt the roles of risk manager and product controller.

Why don't I just use historical data to position size?

In an age where it's increasingly popular to teach and use historical data in decision making, I am a relatively lonely voice in my use of a more flexible, proactive approach. It's now common for traders to believe that by scanning through historical data we can work out risk and reward and where our stop loss levels and so on should be. It's even presented as a way of using real information for our decisions rather than individual judgements; surely this must be better.

Well, I obviously disagree, and the reasons for that are grounded in my belief that historical data is just that: historical. We can only learn what would have happened if we'd actually traded during the period we study, and any observations or judgements that we make will only have relevance in the future if the future exactly mirrors the past; this is almost impossible. The belief that trade analysis based on historical data is somehow more robust is false. So many times I've heard traders say something along the lines of 'I have run this trade through six months' data and so I know what the risks and rewards are'. This type of statement is wrong: the trader can only know the risks and rewards that are portrayed in the data he has examined. For example, just because a stock hasn't fallen by 3 per cent in a day over that period does not mean it can't fall by that amount in the future. But our trader will ignore that possibility because it has not occurred. Similarly, if the period he examined was one of low volatility then he will enter a trade accordingly, whereas he should be trying to judge what the future volatility might be, which will include an analysis of what events, data, and so on are coming up.

So the approach that I favour is initiated by what is happening now and then encompasses what could happen over the coming period. It's not anchored on past results or prices, and so can include a wider range of possible outcomes. Hopefully you can see the difference between what I suggest and the historical data–type approach.

The reality is that no analysis can accurately tell us how the future will unfold; that is all part of the randomness that we must embrace as traders. However, I will always strongly favour approaches that include an attempt at weighing up future outcomes rather than simply analysing the past. Unfortunately, in a technological age, markets are increasingly being seen as a kind of problem that can be solved by maths or data mining, which of course they aren't.

Entering a trade

Once we have conducted our analysis and decided to enter a trade, the next decision is when to do so and at what price. This is an area I believe many retail traders and their educators overcomplicate, typically to their detriment. Before I explain my strategy, I think it will be useful to discuss the approach that is common among private traders, and in particular the technical analysts who educate them.

Once a trend or trade has been identified it is suggested that we look for an entry point; this will typically be related to a technical analysis or chart level. Let's say we want to buy contract FGH. We are typically offered two scenarios. First, we might be told to wait until the price drops slightly and buy on the dip as a way of getting into the trade at a better price. The second approach (the one we need usually depends on what type of graph we are looking at) is to sit and wait for the FGH to rise through a particular level, possibly a resistance level or a breakout of a pattern or trendline, and we should then buy after the breakout. This, we are told, gives us more certainty. Both approaches are essentially based on technical analysis views, and the underlying principle behind both is to improve our chances of success.

The first and easiest point for me to make is that technical analysis and its patterns, lines and levels are nowhere near as reliable as their supporters claim. Indeed I would classify them as being unreliable. I would say that is reason enough not to use them. But let's look at these techniques from both a psychological and market analysis perspective.

When we look at the information from markets and weigh up the various risks and rewards of a trade, we are doing so using the current price information. We cannot weigh up the risks and rewards of a trade with a possible entry price lower or higher at a possible time in the future, because we don't know if even such a situation will exist.

Now let's imagine that we are the trader who has weighed up the information available and decides to buy FGH, but we're waiting to buy on a dip. To me this is absurd; we want to buy a contract because we think it will rise, yet we are going to wait until it falls. Let's say that over the next couple of days FGH does fall and is now at our level; wouldn't we be concerned as to why FGH has now fallen? We should be looking into why a contract that we thought would rise is actually falling; perhaps something has changed.

But what happens if FGH does rally while we are left waiting to buy at a lower level? How would we feel? To put ourselves into a situation where we think that a contract will rise, but we will only look to buy if it falls, is an odd scenario to say the least. I don't like the psychological implications of this approach; there is almost an element of second-guessing or double-bluffing going on.

The alternative technique we are told is that we wait for a higher price level to break and then we buy. But, again, from a psychological and market analysis perspective I don't understand this. Using this method, we make our own judgement that FGH should rally, yet we wait for others to go out and buy it and drive the price higher and only then do we buy. I don't understand why we would do this. We have essentially given up some of our profit, potentially a good deal of it; we have given up our edge and will now be latecomers to the trade. I would be more than a little annoyed that I didn't buy when I originally wanted to. Does buying at a higher price give us a better probability of success? I have seen no evidence of this. If your analysis is correct, then buying at a lower price will obviously be more profitable, and if you're wrong you have a stop loss level to minimise losses.

These ideas, based as they are on technical analysis beliefs, are forms of what professional traders refer to as 'finessing'. Many a trade has been missed by traders trying to finesse the entry point or second-guess the market. These strategies are employed by traders who are unwilling to make their own decisions, and wait for others to act before they trade. This is not the trait of a successful trader; good traders need to think and act independently. If you always need to ask others or wait for others to act, then you are unlikely to become a successful trader, as I explain in chapter 2. Such traders are giving away edge every time they trade, and we simply cannot afford to keep giving away edge if we are to enjoy sustainable profits.

Trading techniques such as these are born not only out of technical analysis but also from the desire to tell traders that they can all be right. The philosophy is that you may not be able to be early on a trade, but even if you are late or delay the trade you can become a profitable trader. I do not concur; I would rather not be in a trade than be late to it. In order to make consistent profits we need to be *earlier* to trades than others. Latecomers will typically 'enjoy' a few small profits but suffer several large losses (the severity of which can make stop loss levels ineffective as the market rapidly goes through them). Indeed, many of the studies of technical analysis indicators, tools and levels that I assessed in *Technical Analysis and the Active Trader* actually showed this pattern of outcomes for those who employ these methods.

So what do I suggest as an entry point? My answer is actually quite simple. When we assess the information at hand and weigh up the risks and reward on a trade, we are doing so using the current information. If I decide this morning that I want to buy FGH, then I will do so this morning at the current price. As a trader I analyse the information as I see it, and then I will find out if my analysis is good. If I buy FGH and it falls, then I am either wrong or early and I must exit the trade. If I am continually wrong in my decisions then I must understand that trading is not for me. I always have a stop loss in place and so if I'm wrong it won't hurt me too much. If I believe that my analysis gives me edge over some participants and I am correct, then I need to act on it and I will be rewarded.

In chapter 1 I explain that in every market that I have traded, the majority of the big orders from bank and hedge-fund traders are executed either before the market opens or in the early period of trading. This is primarily because these professional traders are entering trades in a similar way to the one I have described. Their analysis suggests that they should enter or exit a trade, so if they're right they need to get in before others do.

Just imagine if, during the morning pre-market meeting, a bank trader announced or was instructed to buy a particular contract but, rather than buying when the market opened, he decided to wait to see what happened. The contract rallied and it's now mid-morning and he still hasn't bought it. He's going to have a very difficult conversation with his head trader as to why he hasn't entered the trade and isn't already generating a profit. A reply of 'I was waiting to see what everyone else would do' is likely to anger his seniors even more.

Educated traders will not wait for others to act, because they will always be giving away edge. Besides, our decisions are already based on the actions of many participants over many different markets through looking at the watchlists. The psychology of my type of decision making is that all decisions are the trader's, and the trader must take all responsibility.

The better traders are also not trying to play a fifty–fifty game of wins and losses; they believe and expect that their knowledge and analysis will provide a greater number of winning trades, hence they back their judgement. Having a stop loss and cutting the trade for a small loss, if needed, is their protection from being wrong. The reality is that if they cut losses quickly and run profits, then even a fifty–fifty split of winners and losers can be sufficient.

It is possible that we might be early on a trade and that we enter the trade and get stopped out for a small loss. Exiting the trade does not have to be the end of the idea. We can continue to monitor the market, and if the information remains the same or even improves for the trade, then we can re-enter it. Potentially we can incur one or even two small losses of, say 2 per cent, before re-entering the trade and making, say, 10 per cent. It's important to state, though, that the reason we cut the trade for a small loss is to defend ourselves against the possibility that we are wrong.

Setting targets and stop loss levels

As with the analysis that underpins position sizing, I do not believe we should rely on past data alone to determine our targets and stop loss levels. Again our analysis must start with the current situation and then incorporate the possible future outcomes that we can weigh up. As we are traders as opposed to investors, we will usually hold positions for a relatively short amount of time, typically a few days, or perhaps weeks at most. Therefore, when setting a target we need to understand what type of target is achievable in the time that we are holding the trade. In addition we will understand the context of the current situation and the magnitude of correlated markets from our watchlists, and this will assist too. For example, if you're trading gold shares and its related markets, such as the gold price, are rallying sharply, then you will have a different expectation of target than if the price of gold was rallying to a smaller degree. Of course we also need to factor in what is being priced in, and potential data and so on and these too can lead us to different expectations of a target. So future expectations of volatility and potential price ranges are important, and I explain more about this in chapter 9.

Again, my approach is proactive and means that we set different targets each time we trade because the market situation will be different each time we trade. As with most aspects of trading, we will not become experts at this overnight, and experience will improve our decision making and analysis. However, once again, this is where being a specialist helps, as specialists' more in-depth knowledge of their markets provides them with edge and will greatly help analysis such as target setting. If I were to try to set a target for a trade in a market that I have never traded before then I would find it far more difficult than for a market that I was experienced and knowledgeable in.

Once we have a target in mind, setting the stop loss level is easy; we simply set a level that provides us with a good risk/reward. For example, if I have a target of 8 per cent, then I would want a risk/reward ratio of at least three or four to one and so might set a stop loss level of 2 per cent, thereby risking 2 per cent to make 8 per cent. What I then need to do, particularly if I'm using leverage, is to apply the stop loss level to my trading size and ensure that, overall, I'm not risking more than 1 to 2 per cent of my overall capital.

For example, if I had a $50 000 trading account and with leverage decided to use $40 000 on a trade, I would first set my target: let's say I expect 9 per cent. Next, I would need to set a stop loss, which in this case would be a percentage of the 9 per cent that gave me a good risk/reward; here I would probably use 2 per cent. This 2 per cent of the $40 000 trading size equates to $800, or 1.6 per cent of my overall $50 000 trading account. If my rule was to risk no more than 1.5 per cent of my capital per trade, I would need to amend either the trading size or the stop loss level; in this instance I would probably reduce the trading size. If my rule was to risk no more than 2 per cent, then this trade would be fine.

So my targets and stop loss levels are in no way influenced by past levels or patterns; they are not, therefore, anchored by historical data or an expression of the representative bias. Many other forms of setting targets and stops, such as using support, resistance or pattern levels, are simply short cuts based on unreliable heuristics. While it does take more knowledge and thought to decide upon the targets that I set, this longer thought process that engages our System 2 is exactly what is required to overcome our heuristics. Every trade and every decision must be backed by its own individual assessment, and by definition we cannot use short cuts, biases or heuristics to do this. Of course this is not a 'scientific' approach—but trading is not a science. While it involves numbers it's not a mathematical problem, because there is so much psychology involved; the numbers alone don't tell the whole story.

There is an added benefit to using our own analysis to generate our targets and stop loss levels, which is that our levels will not be easily seen or targeted by other traders, particularly the professionals. One of the common problems with using support, resistance, chart pattern and other technical analysis–based levels is that they are easily understood and known to other traders. Professional futures traders hunt down and trigger technical analysis levels, basically because it's easy to do so. One of the constant issues for technical traders to deal with is trying to find levels that relate to their analysis but are hard for professionals to spot; they often fail in this regard. If our trades do not use these anchors, then we are more likely to be trading under the radar of the professionals, so we can go about our business without fear of being targeted. If you want to be a hunter it's best to be camouflaged; if you're easily spotted, you're more likely to be the prey than the predator.

Pros and cons of small stop loss orders

A common criticism of small stop loss levels is that market volatility can easily take us out of the trade. I know of many traders and educators who employ stop loss levels of 20 per cent or even more. The first point in defence of small losses is simply that small losses will prevent large ones, and if you can cut out large losses then your trading career will be easier.

129

Second, stop loss levels must offer a good risk/reward relative to the target. If you set a stop loss level of say, 10 per cent, then you must expect a profit of 30 per cent or more. Profits such as these are very unlikely for short-term traders; they are likely to take several weeks, usually months, to achieve. As discussed already, trading over these longer horizons is more difficult and is less likely to be based on information; often they are noise trades. If you're risking 10 per cent to make 10 per cent, then it should be clear that you are not trading with edge and are unlikely to enjoy a sustainable trading career.

Larger stop loss levels and longer term trading raises another problem: the possibility that the trade sits at a loss, say 5 per cent or even more, for several weeks or longer, thereby using up trading capital. This capital could either be used for other, more profitable trades, or could even be sitting in a deposit-bearing account earning some interest. What if we had two or three of these trades sitting there, not triggering our stop loss level and not making profit either? This is trading purgatory.

In simple terms, if I conduct my analysis and form the opinion that contract FGH should rise by around 8 per cent and it actually falls 2 cent, then I must be either wrong or early. Two per cent is actually a decent move for any contract; it can usually only do that if there is quite substantial interest that way. If we return to the broker from the early chapters who bought shares only to see them fall by around 20 per cent: how could he still claim to be right? Remember, we only get paid on our views if the market agrees with them. Understanding what other market participants might do is a fundamental aspect of our decision making.

Going back to what I learned during the crash of the Nikkei, if I only hold winners I should only make money. If I hold trades that are losing 5 or 10 per cent or worse without triggering a stop loss, then every day I will need to face those trades again; every day I will need to re-evaluate whether I want to have them; every day I will face the psychological trauma, the cognitive dissonance of a decision that I cannot be sure is correct. This cannot be a good place to be and is, in my opinion, likely to make a long-term trading career more difficult. We need to eliminate as much mental anguish as possible.

I have heard it argued that cutting a trade only to see it perform well would surely cause anguish. This would possibly be true but, as I stated earlier in this chapter, when we exit a trade it does not necessarily mean the end. There is the possibility that we were early and so we can still monitor it and re-enter if the information suggests so. By using a risk/reward of three or four to one, we provide the opportunity to lose once or twice but still make an overall profit if successful on even the third occasion.

Activating a stop loss

When dealing with stop loss levels, another common question is whether to enter a stop loss order into the market or to monitor the market and activate the trade ourselves. The benefit of leaving a stop loss order in the market is that we do not have to continually monitor the market, and it eliminates the chances of forgetting or ignoring the stop loss trade. The downside of leaving the stop loss order is that it may need to be adjusted as the trade moves; it's sometimes more costly in terms of commissions (depends on the product and broker); and sometimes it can lead to poor executions when the level only trades in a small amount.

This last point again raises the issue of how long we spend on trading. A trader who monitors the markets for longer and during market hours has the opportunity to spot the occasions when their stop loss level might only trade in a small size before moving back towards break-even. They may well decide in this instance not to trigger the stop loss trade. By watching the markets in live time they can decide to execute the stop loss trade only if the level starts trading actively. A trader who simply gives the order to a broker or enters it as a stop loss order will almost certainly get filled even on a small trade at the level, and these are the times when traders can get angry at their stop loss trades. As I stated in the early chapters, if you put less time into trading you may have to take some inferior outcomes. These are the kinds of small differences in profit and loss that can compound over the course of a trading year. There is no short cut through this; it's simply a factor of the time we have.

My preference is to monitor the trade and execute the stop loss trade if and when I see good volume at the price. I am confident that I have the discipline to do so, and you should only decide to use this method if you are sure you are disciplined.

Managing trades

Once we have a trade there are some guiding principles to follow in terms of monitoring the position. The first issue is that of cutting losses, which I have already covered. No matter what our analysis tells us, if the trade hits our stop loss level, we should exit. We must have the humility to believe that we can be wrong rather than the arrogance to think the market must be wrong.

When we have a position in the market we should re-evaluate the trade every day, but in the context of what our watchlist is telling us. What I mean by this is that it is crucial that we continue to make objective decisions—but this can be more difficult when we already have a position. As I discuss in chapter 2, traders can have a tendency to cling to an opinion and miss disconfirming evidence. So we employ the disciplines that I explained: we must objectively look at our watchlist each day and essentially ask ourselves, 'What position should I have today?' Or, put another way, 'If I had no position what trade would I want?' For some this will undoubtedly be easier said than done, but this is the mindset that we must adopt. We need to weigh up what we would do if we didn't have the position. If the answer is that we would enter the trade, then we can keep our existing trade. But if the information has changed, then so too must our decision; remember, 'When the facts change so do I'.

This is another area where understanding the context of our trade can be a great help, because we should know when the context or market conditions have changed. If originally all of the markets on our watchlist pointed one way but now there is an even split, then clearly conditions have changed. It might even be possible that we should completely reverse the trade; certainly we need to keep that in mind as a possibility. We must never become too attached to any trade; we must do what our analysis tells us and not be unduly influenced by our original decision.

As well as the trade itself, we also need to re-evaluate our targets and stop loss levels. Again, by understanding the current market conditions and what they were when we entered the trade, we can and should make adjustments to both when required. This is a continuation of the proactive approach that I favour; changing our trade to suit the market conditions rather than simply trying to run the same trade even as conditions change.

Our goal is to run profits as long as possible without taking undue risk. I believe it's preferable to exit and re-enter the same trade several times over a period of months rather than hold it on the occasions that it starts to go against us. It's only in hindsight that we know that a trade has recovered after it has triggered a stop loss order. By exiting the trade when it goes against us and triggering our stop loss, we are passing the risk to another trader. We will only get back in if our information tells us to do so, and we must not be worried about getting back in at a price that is worse than we previously exited at. If we have selected a good broker then we will be paying low commissions, so we should not be concerned about that. If we are good at our job we will predominantly be generating commissions to make profits, so we should not fear them.

In keeping with the proactive and flexible approach, we do not simply have to keep the original trade and can adjust the position size if market conditions change. We do this in line with the situations that I explained earlier in the chapter. So, for example, if volatility starts to rise but the trade still looks good we can decide to reduce the position size. Or if we start with a smaller position size we can add to it as the trade and information improves.

From time to time we are faced with what I term 'bonus profits'. This is when we enter a trade, let's say with an 8 per cent target, and very quickly the contract moves significantly more in our favour, in this instance say 20 per cent. The information may still be positive and we have decided to stay in the trade and increase both our target and our trailing stop. However, even with these adjustments I suggest selling part of the position at this price; professional traders often call this 'making a print' at the new price. While we want to run profits as long as possible, this move was an unexpected bonus.

Years of experience and tens of thousands of trades have shown me that sometimes there can be a sharp retracement after such moves. So, in part, the reduction in trading size is related to the increase in volatility, but there is also a psychological aspect to this; how would we feel if the next day the contract did retrace and we had to give back much of our profit? By selling some of the position, if it keeps rallying we are still in the trade, but if it does retrace we will be happy that we exited some at the better level. We are trying to protect ourselves from potential mental anguish by covering for both eventualities (the idea is similar to hedging). By making a print we are trying to ensure that, whatever happens over the next few days, we will exit the trade in profit. If we keep the whole trade and there is a sharp retracement that leads to our stop loss order being executed significantly lower than we wanted then, we risk losing most or all of our profit.

Moves such as these are unlikely to be seen in backtesting, so trying to find the 'optimum' solution is virtually impossible. We must remember that the best course of action is usually only found in hindsight, which is partly why at the time of each trade we need to look ahead to what could happen and weigh up the various outcomes. This is part of the art or skill of trading; it is not a scientific profession, despite attempts to portray it that way.

Trailing stops

It's crucial to keep a trailing stop loss order for winning trades. As the trade makes money we increase (for long positions) and decrease (for short trades) the stop loss level so that we protect most of the profits that we have generated. If a trade is making say, 5 per cent, we do not want to give even half of that back. So whereas the original stop loss might have been at −2 per cent, our new stop loss level may be at +3 per cent, or 2 per cent below the current price. Giving up profits is almost as great a sin as not cutting losses.

This links to another important psychological aspect: always keeping your positions marked to the current market price and, importantly, making that new price the reference point in your decision making. Almost all brokers and/or exchanges ensure that your positions will be marked to the new market price each day and that your account will reflect gains or losses accordingly. However, many traders continue to view the trade in their mind according to the entry price; this is a mistake. Once we have a position, whatever the new market price is each day, *that* is the price at which we now own the trade. Any profit that has been generating by a winning trade has done so because of the new price, and any movement away from that price against us will effectively cause us losses — our account value will drop.

In gambling, the casino is referred to as the 'house', and money won from the casino is termed 'house money'. It has been well documented by psychologists that people are more willing to gamble with 'house money' than with the money they brought with them. It's as if this money isn't really theirs, it's a bonus that they are happier to play with as opposed to their own 'hard earned' money, which they may think more carefully about.

The reason I refer to 'house money' is because if you refer to a winning position by the entry price, it's more likely that you will view the profits as 'house money' and possibly gamble it away. Whereas if you use today's price for winning trades, then all profits are yours and any move against you from today's price will be rightly viewed in terms of being a loss.

I have seen so many traders and, in particular, investors give up huge sums by continuing to view their positions by the entry price. I spoke to someone recently who had bought shares in FGE .AU at around 60 cents a few years ago. The stock rallied as high as around $7 before crashing back at one point to 60 cents. At that point he told me that he hadn't lost any money on the trade, whereas I told him that he had lost 90 per cent of what had. That's quite a difference of opinion, and a difference in his account too! (Post script: FGE ended up going into administration.)

My suggestion in chapter 6 to move funds out of your trading account and into your own account is also a way to combat the 'house money' effect. Once the funds are in your own account it's clear that they are yours, thereby removing any tendency there might be to gamble with trading profits.

So once we have a position, there are a number of scenarios available to us, the main ones being to run the trade until our target is reached, whether that is our initial target or a target that has been changed subsequently; cut the trade for a loss; sell part of the trade, either because of a bonus move or because market conditions have changed; exit all of the trade because conditions have changed; or reverse the position because conditions have changed. Despite what some educators suggest, we will not simply put the trade on then sit back by the pool sipping pina coladas waiting for the profits to enter our account. (Yes, I have actually read statements to that effect!)

You may note that I have not included doubling up on losing positions as a possible scenario, and there is good reason for this—I don't agree with the idea, as it has the real potential to break my first rule: preserving capital. I have known many traders over the years who have used this technique. Some have got away with it (often only just); others have been wiped out. My view is that any technique that has the potential to wipe us out should be excluded from our trading.

The only occasions when I have doubled up on a losing trade have been when the move was quite substantial but was not supported by any information from any other market. On these (rare) occasions I have added to the position, but only looked to break even on the new trade with the lower average cost (that is, I don't try for the home run of turning a large loser into a winner; rather I'm happy to turn it into a break-even). Sometimes, if the move was unsubstantiated, the market can bounce straight back and provide a profit—but this is just a bonus. I never, however, double up if the market slowly grinds against me—this type of move usually has more momentum behind it and I will be stopped out before the loss becomes large and the option to double up presents itself. It can be said that doubling-up is an expression of conservativeness—the tendency for people to cling to an opinion. Rather than accepting and making decisions on what is happening now, by doubling up, a trader is essentially saying that the original trade was right and the market is now wrong; this is a dangerous view and one that also suggests overconfidence.

In general nowadays there has been a move to less flexible and proactive position management, and I know that my views buck this trend. Increasingly, traders are being taught to use predetermined, mechanical or technical approaches—which they are told will eliminate the potential for poor discipline and other psychological weaknesses. However, not only are the technical tools and indicators unreliable, but they are also actually themselves products of our desire for short cuts.

The methods are taught in the belief that anyone can follow them and everyone can become a successful trader. I simply do not believe that, nor have I seen any evidence to support the notion. Rather than lead you on a false path of believing everyone can be profitable, the techniques and disciplines that I have outlined in this chapter are based on the view that some people will be able to apply them better than others; these will be the more successful traders. Today, it seems almost politically incorrect to suggest that some people will be better than others—but this is a fact of life across a wide range of disciplines, skills and, of course, sports. The financial junk-food industry needs as many people as possible to believe that they can be successful, but it's time to cut through that bull.

The underlying aim with all the disciplines that I outline in this chapter is to cut losses and run profits. I am often asked, 'How long do you run trades for?' The answer is, 'As long as possible'. The reality is that holding trades with a tight stop loss for longer than a week or two is usually unlikely. However, it may be that I enter and exit the same trade a number of times. It's also important to keep profits. As the saying goes, 'It is not just about making money; you have to keep it'.

We must try to eliminate psychological short cuts and weaknesses, and I hope to have explained some ways to do that. I am also trying to take you off the psychological roller-coaster that so many traders ride. They swing from big profits to large losses, and that roller-coaster ride will reduce their ability to enjoy a long trading career. Even if they manage to survive financially they will be psychologically battered. I hope to take you off that roller-coaster by employing disciplines that lead to a succession of steady but consistent profits and only small losses. If you don't have to cope with large losses, then your trading mind will be the better for it.

Relating these techniques to our core principles

If we look back to our core principles as stated at the start of part II, you will see that the techniques that I have outlined are consistent with them.

Rule 1 is that we must preserve our capital; by having relatively tight stop losses, and so cutting trades for a small loss, we are meeting this goal.

Rule 2 is that we must be able to trade in as many market conditions as possible; we achieve this by making individual assessments of each trade and each market condition. We therefore adapt our trading size, targets and stop loss levels and position management according to the prevailing market condition. By being flexible in all these areas, we give ourselves a greater chance of being able to trade in various market conditions, including from high to low volatility.

Rule 3 is that it's necessary to understand context; this is achieved by using our watchlists and applying the information that we see. In order to make different decisions for each trade we must have an understanding of current and future context.

Lastly, there is the need to employ our System 2 brain—to think and act more slowly and deliberately. Again, by assessing each trade on its own merits and revisiting every piece of analysis every time we trade, and by omitting the short cuts such as support and resistance levels in our analysis, we are helping to achieve this goal. The analysis that's required to assess a target requires more background knowledge and time to make a judgement. We are not looking for short cuts; in fact we are actively seeking out as much information as possible.

Summary

- Cut losses quickly.
- Employ a flexible, proactive approach to position sizing and trade management.
- Targets and stop levels must reflect good risk/reward.
- Look ahead rather than backwards.
- Re-evaluate objectively.

Part III
The next level: incorporating more advanced concepts

In the previous section of the book I explained some of the fundamental aspects of building a trading career, such as the knowledge required, constructing watchlists and being business-minded. There are no short cuts to finding out whether we can become successful traders; the groundwork needs to be done, and it may take several months until you are confident that you have these fundamental areas covered.

Nowadays, the more common method for retail traders to be taught is to scan and backtest through hundreds of contracts using potentially hundreds of indicators, patterns, and so on, until you find a combination that 'works'. This, it is suggested, gives you edge, which you can then profit from. This type of trading is neither robust nor reliable, and it is unlikely to provide edge. Besides, do you really think that a small retail trader sitting at home on a home PC will find edge scanning through markets that have already been trawled through in much greater depth by hedge funds and investment banks?

In part III I want to expand on some topics that I have already mentioned briefly, including the topics of pricing in and volatility. While these are more advanced subjects, this does not mean that you should avoid considering them in the early days of your trading. They need to be incorporated into your trading from the outset. Whether you are a manual trader or looking to incorporate my ideas into a more automated technique, the topics that I will cover in this section will still apply. In fact, the best automated trading strategies that I have seen do use these ideas; but it does increase the complexity of designing such a tool by a significant degree. Meanwhile, many automated and manual traders continue to ignore topics such as pricing in, either because they are too hard to grasp and incorporate, or simply due to ignorance.

While you will need to include these ideas in your trading from day one, these areas are undoubtedly ones that we will improve upon with experience. We should expect that initially we will not be the best trader we can be; rather we should be looking to improve our decision making, knowledge and analysis over time. Of course, we need to make it to the long run, which means surviving the short term. This, in turn, requires strict discipline, as outlined in chapter 7. The journey of gaining experience and knowledge is an ongoing (never-ending) one that we must enjoy if we are to become successful and have longevity.

The topics covered in this section are in particular the ones that will offer us significant challenges and rewards if we can apply them correctly. They are omitted by many (if not most) traders, so again, those who can incorporate them correctly will gain edge over others. Once again, there are no short cuts here; no indicators or patterns alone can provide a quick, reliable decision-making tool. With these topics we are delving into some of the more complex concepts of trading, but in many ways they also encompass the true essence of how markets work.

For further reading on some of the concepts discussed I would suggest reading Nassim Nicholas Taleb (*Fooled by Randomness* and *Black Swan*) and George Soros (*Alchemy of Finance*). They are, in my opinion, three of the very best trading books ever written.

Chapter 8

Pricing in

In this chapter...

I explain in depth the concept of pricing in that I have alluded to earlier. To many readers this may be a controversial topic but I can assure you that every market professional that I have worked with agrees with this concept. Most of us find it hard to comprehend why the topic of pricing in is either misunderstood or completely ignored by many in the retail side of the industry.

I have a confession to make: in chapter 1 I omit one of the most widespread myths in the industry. It's an assumption that underpins many forms of analysis and forms the foundations of the majority of trading systems and techniques that are taught to private traders. The myth is that the market is ahead.

The idea that the market is ahead is a fundamental principle of technical analysis—if you don't believe it's valid, then you simply should not use technical indicators and patterns. But many 'fundamental'-type traders also believe in this theory, and even many fundamental analysts incorporate key aspects of the theory to their analysis.

By believing that the market is ahead we are making the assumption that the market (or at least most of its participants) 'knows' the outcome. Often this is explained to retail traders through the idea that insider trading is commonplace and we should follow what everyone else is doing. So following the herd or trend has become possibly the most accepted trading technique; if everyone else is buying, then we should do so too, as 'those in the know' must have an idea what the outcome will be.

There are times when we will trade with the herd or the trend, when our information tells us to do so. Further, we should incorporate an aspect of this theory into our trading by using the philosophy that we need to know what others are doing (remember Keynes saying that the market is like a beauty contest where we are trying to guess which beauty everyone else will choose). But, and this is a big but, we also need to incorporate how these traders will react if they're wrong.

This last point is significant, and it's drawn from the view that the market is not ahead; traders do not know the outcome. The alternative view that I suggest is that market participants price in an outcome — they believe that a certain outcome is likely. But they can be wrong and when they are wrong the effect can be substantial. I actually think that most traders and investors are aware that markets can price in the wrong outcome — after all, we often see the effects of a stock not meeting earnings expectations. However, this is still an area that I believe most traders fail to incorporate adequately into their trading.

There are substantial differences between the two theories of 'pricing in' and 'the market is ahead'. The latter is easier to understand, analyse and incorporate into trading, whereas pricing in is far more complex. Believing that the market is ahead suits the financial junk-food industry, as it allows the belief that everyone can profit from trading; all we need to do is either follow the trend or look through past data and/or technical indicators to find something that supposedly tells us what people are doing. As anyone can conduct this type of analysis, this philosophy suits the purposes of the many educators who believe they can teach anyone to become a profitable trader. Obviously, if you want a successful business it's better to create as large a market as possible for your product. Telling everyone that they can become a successful trader, therefore, helps the financial junk-food industry.

If we examine the theory that markets price in outcomes rather than knowing them, then the job of a trader certainly becomes more difficult and possibly falls outside the comfort zone of some. Among other skills, we will need the ability to weigh up outcomes that have not yet occurred; this is not easy, and is one significant area that we will try to improve on with experience. This is part of the art or skill of becoming a good trader, and one reason why not everyone can succeed. If you show two different traders the same information they may well come to two very different conclusions about what can happen next. What I can say, though, is that anyone who bases their decision solely on analysis of past data or charts will only be able to analyse a small sample of potential future outcomes. They can only weigh up the events and outcomes that have occurred in the data they are studying, and they are more likely to be hit by 'unforeseen' events.

I have no doubt that the idea that markets price in outcomes rather than know them is understood and used by many professional traders. Those of us who have traded as market-makers at the heart of markets, able to see how many different types of participants act, see this in action each and every day. As is often the case in this business, though, those who have not witnessed firsthand how different types of traders actually operate form opinions that are not based on reality, but rather are based on rumours or simply on what is easy to explain and implement (a short cut).

To implement the view that markets price in outcomes we need to incorporate two types of analysis into our decision making. The first is to work out what is being priced in, which is the more straightforward aspect to analyse. The second technique is to weigh up possible future outcomes; this can be more difficult. Both manual and automated traders need to include these techniques, but in reality it may be harder for automated traders to do so, because strict rules are hard to construct and program.

Without question, we will not be able to simply employ the tools, indicators and patterns that so many traders use, as they can only shed light on one part of the equation: what the market might be pricing in. The second, crucial, aspect of our decision making, what could happen next, requires deeper thought and knowledge and is one of the only aspects of our trading that will require some subjective analysis.

Let's look at the two techniques required and that analysis needed to conduct them. Firstly, we need to work out what is being priced in to the contract we are investigating. The first step in this analysis is to simply find out what direction the contract has been heading in. Charts can be used here but specialists often do not need to use them; if we are trading a contract that we are specialists in, then we should already have the knowledge. So, in simple terms, if the contract has been rising then it's more likely to be pricing in good news, and vice versa if it's falling. The larger the move the more the market is expecting either positive or negative. Sideways movement indicates a market that has no firm opinion.

As I have already mentioned, many small and mid-cap stocks are not able to be short sold, which means that they can be more prone to exhibit bullish tendencies, particularly ahead of data or news. We need to remember that, in these instances, the share price may not reflect the views of everyone who examines the stock; it only reflects the views of those who are bullish. This will also have a significant influence on our later analysis of weighing up possible future outcomes. Obviously, markets such as currencies, typically don't have the same issues. (The exceptions would be some of the smaller currencies.) So, as with all analysis, working out what is being priced in needs to be conducted in the context of the contract we are looking at. Contrary to what technical analysts tell us, we cannot simply employ the same analysis to every contract.

The next step in working out what is being priced in is to investigate other sources of information about participants' positioning. This is not available for all products, for example currencies, but some contracts do offer us some further information if we take the time to look. Futures exchanges, for example, provide data of Open Interest, which is the quantity of current open positions. By tracking this we can see if new positions are being opened during a move (Open Interest will increase) or if instead traders are closing out trades, in which case we would see Open Interest fall.

For some share markets we can investigate the quantity of short positions, knowing that a huge majority of share market participants only trade from the long side (they only buy shares). For most shares we should expect to see short sale interest at less than 1 or 2 per cent, remembering too that many smaller stocks are not able to be short sold. If we see short interest at levels in excess of, say, 5 per cent, then this is quite a substantial number of traders trading from the short side and suggests that a significant number of participants are expecting bad news and/or data. Part of being a specialist is that by routinely examining this type of information we'll develop a good idea of what is 'normal' for our market and when conditions have changed. Once again, it is through knowledge and use of market data that we can create edge over others and improve our understanding and analysis of the products that we trade.

Examination of derivative products can sometimes provide useful information, and it should be included in our routine. However, not all products have listed derivatives or transparent derivative information. Predominantly we are looking at options' Open Interest when examining derivatives and we are seeking out whether any particular options type or strike price has larger-than-normal open positions. Options analysis will require an understanding of options and, again, we see the benefit of knowledge — traders who don't understand options will see less information and find fewer trades than traders who do.

So, having analysed how participants are positioned, the next step is to weigh up possible outcomes. This will involve both working out what could happen if the market is correct, but also what could happen if what is being priced in doesn't eventuate — that is, if the market is wrong. As discussed earlier, it's this second stage that most traders fail to include in their analysis.

Our watchlists will be suggesting a certain direction for us to trade. For example, if we're trading gold shares we may have overwhelming information pointing to a rally. However, before we commit to a long position we also need to understand how the market is positioned and we might need to adjust our position accordingly. In particular we need to be aware if any data is expected in the coming period, because these are times when sharp moves can occur.

Markets are like a roulette table, where participants are constantly placing their bets as to what might happen — this is how pricing in works. Data and news flows are like the ball dropping on the roulette table; it's when participants find out if they are right. The difference between markets and roulette is, first, there are really only two possible outcomes for traders—up or down—rather than the 32 for roulette players. Second, the payoff for traders is often not the same for each of the two outcomes. If the market is generally positioned for good news and the data is indeed good, then often the payout can be small; that is, the rally is small because the good news has already been priced in. However, if the market is braced for good news and in fact the data is bad, then the resulting fall can be quite severe. The risk/reward of this type of situation can be skewed quite significantly, hence the importance of analysing these possible outcomes before they occur.

This last point relates back to a quote that I used early on, which remains one of the best pieces of advice ever given to me: 'You will make the most money when you have the opposite position to everyone else.' These are the times when the market is positioned one way and the outcome is not as expected. It's vital that our trading includes the ability to foresee such events and position accordingly.

While many pieces of data and company earnings are scheduled in advance, thereby giving us the chance to prepare for them, the reality is that news is hitting the markets each and every day. This is part and parcel of the randomness that is undoubtedly an ingredient of this business. You may well ask: If there's so much randomness, aren't we just wasting our time trying to trade? To answer, first we need to accept and embrace the randomness rather than fight it or claim we can ever master it. Things will happen that we could not have foreseen. Some will help and some will hurt; we cannot foresee everything and we cannot trade every move. Again, this is a different philosophy from the new norm whereby traders are told they can find an indicator to trade any market; these trading styles rely on hindsight to trade and, while we can always find trades in hindsight, they were not predictable ahead of the move.

Second, we are obviously predominantly concerned with adverse effects from the random events—surprising losses are obviously of far more concern than unexpected profits. However, if we investigate and weigh up what is being priced in and what could possibly hurt that prevailing mood, we will be factoring unexpected events into our thinking. Every time we trade we need to ask, 'What could happen if the market is wrong?' Whether we trade with the market (trend) or against it, we must ask this question. While we can prepare for scheduled data, by asking this question every day we will also be planning for unexpected events. The point is that the most damaging moves are when the market is wrong, so we must always include that analysis in our trading.

There have been a number of occasions during my career when I have entered a trade that is contrary to the prevailing trend, sometimes because there was some information, sometimes because I believed the market was positioned too heavily and there was scope for the market to be wrong. These trades are usually put on in smaller size because they are more speculative (as per chapter 7). When they pay off, they do so in a significant way (so the smaller position size is compensated for). More often than not, it's some unexpected news that caused the market reversal and the profit for my trade. I have often been asked by other traders, 'How did you know that was going to happen?' The reality is that I didn't know what news was going to come out, if any at all; I simply positioned myself according to the market conditions that I saw.

This type of analysis is similar to the technique of looking for disconfirmation that I explained is so critical to our decision making. In this instance we are concerned with investigating why the market might be wrong, in addition to our usual investigation of why our trade might be incorrect. I cannot place too much emphasis on the need to understand and incorporate these techniques. Of course those who believe the market is ahead, and so follow the lead of others in the belief they know the outcome, will not, by definition, be investigating why or how the market could be wrong.

The assumption that the market is ahead is obviously a pure contradiction to the view that the market can be wrong and the theory of pricing in. Ultimately we must all choose which we believe is the more robust theory (there are no laws in this regard, only theories) but I would say that a large majority of traders with experience at the heart of markets will favour pricing in. If you are in any doubt, I will shortly show some examples that help to disprove the theory that markets are ahead and support the hypothesis that markets price in expectations.

What is good (bad) news?

Before progressing with some examples, it's important to explain what I mean by good and bad news, as this is an area of confusion for many private traders and commentators. Typically, these two groups refer to good and bad news in the context of analysts' expectations, but this is naive and omits market positioning. We should be more concerned with the market's expectations as shown by how participants have positioned themselves.

For example if, in the run up to its earnings report, a stock has rallied quite sharply, then we should conclude that the market is expecting better results than the analysts' view. Similarly, a fall in advance of data suggests the market is more bearish than the forecasts. This type of positioning creates situations such as when a stock meets the analysts' forecasts but still falls, usually confusing commentators and many traders and investors.

So there is a difference between analysts' expectations and market expectations; while we need to investigate both, it's the market's expectations that are of more concern to our analysis, as this is where the real money is made or lost. The same analysis of data is used for economic figures, too, if you are trading currencies or bonds, for example. Please note that, particularly with company announcements, there can also be extra information to the earnings that may contain more clear-cut good or bad news, such as improvements or deterioration of trading conditions.

Examples

The following examples are shown as much to nullify the case for markets being ahead as to support the hypothesis that markets price in outcomes and can be wrong. They are all Australian stocks taken from the end of 2013.

QBE Insurance

First let's examine QBE.AU, an insurance stock, in the run-up to its earnings report at the end of 2013. Figure 8.1 is the chart of QBE.

Figure 8.1: QBE Insurance chart

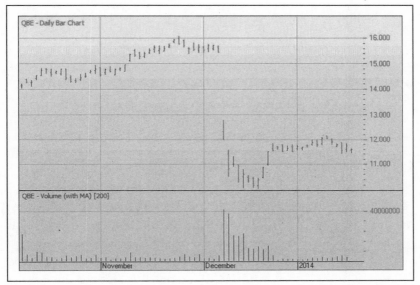

As we can see in the run-up to its earnings announcement in early December 2013, QBE's share price was quite buoyant, rallying from $14 to just under $16 in two months. Investigation of the outstanding short positions (published by the Australian Securities and Investments Commission, ASIC) showed that less than 1 per cent of the stock had been short sold. So we can deduce that the market was quite comfortable-to-bullish about QBE, with very few traders believing a fall was likely; this stock was pricing in good news.

As you will see, QBE announced bad figures that missed both analysts' and market expectations — so severe that the shares fell by around 25 per cent, a significant move for such a large-cap stock.

The first point that we can make is that the market was not ahead, and those who had bought in the run-up to the figures did not know the outcome. In fact they were proved massively wrong, and if you'd followed the trend you would have suffered severe losses. I'll repeat here that every technical analysis–based technique, whether it's indicators, moving averages or chart patterns, is based on the assumption that the market is ahead — if you don't believe that assumption, you should not use these tools.

While we could not have known what the data was going to be, it would have been possible for us to conclude that the market was pricing in good news. Anyone trading QBE around this time would need to weigh up the potential effects of both good and bad news. With good news already factored into the price, a good piece of data would have to be significantly better than analysts' expectations to even justify the rally, let alone spark a further rise.

As the earnings report was a scheduled update, we could have planned and incorporated this into our trading. The fact is that a vast majority of participants in this stock did not conduct such analysis (or the stock would have fallen more in the run-up to the data as they unwound risk). So a trader who does include the pricing in analysis and weighs up possible outcomes, including the market being wrong, will clearly have edge over others in this market. This is a clear example of when we can make a lot of money by having the opposite position to the crowd. Placing that kind of trade requires the ability to think and act independently; it requires us to sometimes trade against the trend. If you are uncomfortable with that, then you will miss many of the best trades.

Note also how the magnitude of the fall had not been experienced by the stock for at least several months previously (in fact, for longer than is shown on this graph), so this is an outcome that a backtester would not have been able to factor into their analysis. Even a knowledgeable trader who incorporates market positioning may not have weighed up the possibility of a 25 per cent fall, but it would have been possible to weigh up the possibility of a 10+ per cent fall given the market positioning, even though such a move had not shown up on previous data. If the market was wrong in its upbeat opinion we could have expected the stock to give up a good part at least of its recent gains. This is why traders who believe that they can weigh up all risks and rewards of a system through backtesting are incorrect; they can only weigh up what has previously occurred, and hence they are often overconfident in their analysis.

I know that I cannot weigh up every single possible outcome, but I also know that I am weighing up a lot more alternatives than most traders. Importantly, I am weighing up outcomes that may not have occurred in the past.

Iluka

Iluka (ILU.AU) is a mineral sands miner with, I think it is fair to say, a chequered share-price history. Like many mining firms it can be prone to large swings in its fortunes. So let's look at ILU from the perspective of market positioning. Its share price is shown in figure 8.2.

Figure 8.2: Iluka chart

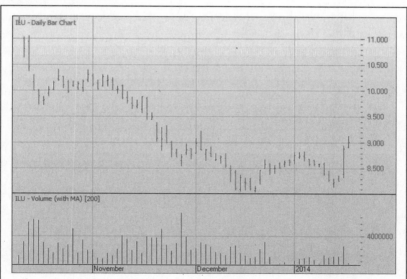

Iluka's earnings announcement came out in mid January 2014, so we need to examine the period before then. It's clear that in terms of performance the stock had been falling for a while, suggesting that the market was expecting another poor report from Iluka after previous weak figures earlier in 2013. Analysis of the short-selling situation from just before the announcement shows that almost 10 per cent of the stock was short sold; that is a very high figure and suggests that a significant number of traders were bearish on the stock. So analysis of this stock just prior to its earnings would have shown that the market was pricing in weak data.

Given what was being priced in, it wouldn't take too much to drive this stock higher; even figures that were in line with analysts' expectations would be ahead of what the market was factoring in. This is in fact what happened: a decent, if not great, report was met with a sharp rally (the second-last bar on the right of figure 8.2) as the market had been caught on the wrong side. The stock had been falling and there were significant short positions, a perfect environment for a sharp rally. As we would have known that an earnings report was due, a good trader could have seen this as an opportunity for a move; it would be the time when the market finds out if it's correct in its views. As with QBE, the market was wrong.

If we again weigh up what could happen if the market was right or wrong, we should conclude that a weak report would need to be very weak to send the stock down further, whereas a report of in-line or better could spark a rally. The expected return would favour being long, even though the trend is lower.

Once again, we should see that before embarking on a trade it's vital to conduct analysis of how participants are currently positioned. If other information had been suggesting we should be short ILU, then market-positioning analysis would have served up contrarian evidence. Remember that we do not know what the data will be, but we try to position ourselves for the best expected return. A short trade might deliver a gain of, say 5 per cent, but a long trade could expect to make 10 per cent or more; if data is a fifty-fifty probability (and I would say in this instance it is actually slanted in favour of a rally) then the expected return favours a long trade.

It is also worth referring back to the myth that traders can ignore data. Like many of the other myths and short cuts, this one is born from the false belief that the market is ahead; 'Just follow the others and don't worry about the data because the market knows' is the mantra from the financial junk-food industry. The reality is that data is very important to markets and we need to understand the relationship between market positioning and data, the concept of pricing in. The moves that we have seen with ILU and QBE are significant and they are unquestionably data-driven; it is folly to ignore data.

Probability and magnitude

Many courses and trading educators teach methods based on backtesting and probability. We are told to mine through historical data or charts and look for trading strategies or indicators that have a high probability of success. I have already explained at length the problems associated with backtesting but I now want to briefly take on the topic of probability. The issue of probability in trading is more complex than is widely taught and accepted, for the probability of success is only one part of the equation. As the Iluka and QBE examples clearly show, the potential magnitude of outcomes is equally as important as the probability of their occurrence.

To work out that a trade has a fifty-fifty chance of success is meaningless without attaching magnitude. What if there was a 50 per cent chance of a 5 per cent rally and a 50 per cent chance of a 10 per cent fall? The expected return favours a fall despite there being a 50 per cent chance of both outcomes. A 70 per cent chance of a market rallying means nothing if the magnitude of the possible fall is three times greater. Here a trade with a 30 per cent probability would still have a higher expected return than the 70 per cent probability trade.

Of course, I dispute the probability figures themselves that are mined from backtesting and, additionally, backtesting cannot provide the full range of possible magnitudes. However, so many traders use a simplistic probability approach in the false belief that high probability puts them on the right side of a trade. On so many levels, that type of trading includes poor assumptions.

Pricing in and position sizing

The concept of pricing in is just one of the types of analysis that we must incorporate into our decision making. It's easier to demonstrate the idea at times of data, but we must use pricing in analysis at all times. After the examples given, I would imagine that some readers might be thinking, 'Why not just develop a trading strategy around times of data and buy contracts that have been sold heavily, and short sell contracts that have been bought up?' The answer is that we can have no idea of how many losing trades we will have before we get a winner. Each trade is independent of each other and, even if the expected return of each is positive, it's possible to sustain four, five, six or more losses before a winner. Even if the losses were small, say 2 or 3 per cent, a winner would need to be very large to compensate. Such a system would be a rule-of-thumb method, and too simplistic for my liking. You can end up trading contracts that you know little about and may miss some other information. I believe it's preferable to include this analysis with the techniques explained earlier to enhance your specialisation; this is how we build significant edge. Remember too, that we must treat each trade and each day as a unique situation and judge each on its own merits as objectively as possible. Pre-determined trades are typically short cuts.

There will, though, be some occasions when we want to act on market positioning analysis alone. For example, if you are trading insurance stocks as a sector and believe that the possibility of QBE failing to meet expectations provides a good expected return for a short sell trade. It's important to view this type of trade as a speculative one and to therefore use a smaller position size. We don't want to try and develop our trading around this type of situation alone, but it can provide opportunities from time to time.

Market positioning analysis may also cause us to reduce our position size for a trade where we otherwise have strong or overwhelming information. For example, our watchlists suggest we should be long gold stocks, but we are concerned that the market is pricing in quite good news already. We may therefore decide to reduce the trade size. Alternatively we can choose to use options for the trade; in this instance we might buy call options that have a defined risk. If the market positioning is extremely one-way and if we know there is data due out then we would likely decide against the trade.

This raises an interesting point of difference between me and many retail traders. For me, one of the most worrying positions to be in is to have the same position as most of the market, because I know that if the market and I are wrong then the loss will be significant. In the instances when I have such a trade I will be even more vigilant than usual in seeking disconfirming evidence. However, most retail traders and investors that I know take comfort in trading with the herd, believing that if so many others agree then they must be right. Of course, as we now know, the market is not always ahead, and I take no comfort in losing if everyone else is too.

Strong trends and bubble-type environments are actually very hard to trade once we add pricing in into our analysis. This is an area where ignorance is bliss (for a while) for most traders—they go with strong trends believing that market forces are with them, but ultimately they are likely to get burned. The problem we face during bubble-type situations (such as the dotcom share bubble) is that the profitable way to trade is to go along with the bubble—trying to short into it would result in constant losses. We have to trade the environment we see, but sometimes that environment will be a worrying one to go along with. We would expect the bubble to end at some point and the correction to be sharp and substantial. This is another example of when we would need to use smaller position sizing, but understanding the bubble context of the time we might be ready to go short when the bubble bursts. Importantly, we would not look to add to long positions during a fall. As always, an understanding of context is vital before we commit to any trades.

Bubble- or severe bear-type markets can also be recognised by the way that contracts respond to data. If, for example, stocks respond positively to both good and bad data, then they are likely trading in a strong bull or bubble-type market. We need to incorporate this into our analysis and trading. During bull markets, contracts can often ignore bad news and this does pose a problem to more rational and knowledgeable traders. Similarly, during bear markets good news can be ignored. I would suggest from experience that these situations are more likely to be associated with shares rather than other markets. This is a further reason why we should not implement rules-of-thumb such as short selling shares that have risen ahead of data — we need to treat each occasion on its merits.

Reflexivity in markets

When we investigate concepts such as pricing in and market positioning we are delving into the realms of the reflexive nature of markets. To quote from George Soros, who is the predominant advocate of reflexivity:

> Financial markets attempt to predict a future that is contingent on the decisions people make in the present. Instead of just passively reflecting reality, financial markets are actively creating the reality that they, in turn, reflect. There is a two-way connection between present decisions and future events.

In short, reflexivity is the way that our (and the market's) actions will themselves influence the final outcome for that market. So there is no pre-determined outcome as believed by many, including technical analysts. Where the market goes tomorrow and afterwards will be partly the result of what we do today; there is a two-way reflexive nature to markets. Therefore reflexivity fits very well with the concepts of pricing in and market positioning, because they too infer that the way the market is positioned will influence what the final outcome will be. As we saw previously, it's not just data and news that affect a market; it's how the market is positioned that will determine the magnitude and nature of any move.

As already explained, believing in a pre-determined outcome makes life far simpler for both traders and investors, but it's incorrect. I agree wholeheartedly with Soros's concept of reflexivity and, further,

I would suggest that most traders with good market experience (particularly at the centre of markets) will agree with this too.

Analysts both fundamental and technical rarely if ever incorporate the concept of reflexivity into their analysis. Fundamental analysts will look over balance sheets and profit and loss accounts to make forecasts of a market value without regard for how market positioning will affect whether that target can be reached. Technical analysts believe that the market is ahead, which assumes there is a pre-determined outcome, again; incorrect. Some will claim that overbought and oversold indicators incorporate the idea of market positioning but they don't; they're simply short cuts.

Reflexivity (pricing in) is another reason why longer term trading is more difficult than short term. Events many months into the future are dependent on how participants trade along the way. We can't possibly know what will happen in weeks or months to come, let alone know how participants will react to the various events along the way. Today, we can only weigh up how people are positioned today—and all we can do is to examine the information objectively each and every day and update our positioning accordingly.

Conclusion

Due to the complex and conceptual nature of this topic I thought a quick conclusion would be in order.

Pricing in and market positioning undoubtedly increase the level of difficulty of our decision making; there are so many ideas and outcomes to weigh up. However, trying to simplify trading too much will only lead to unreliable or irrational short cuts. We need to trade the markets as they are, not as we would like them to be. While pricing in is a harder concept to incorporate than simply believing the market is ahead, it is how markets operate and therefore we need to include it. My predominant aim is not to make your trading easier or quicker; it's to make it more profitable and consistent.

Another point to take from this topic is to see that trading is not simply a matter of trying to predict market direction; there are times, such as when we are investigating market positioning, when there is a right and a wrong way to position ourselves. If we took a short trade in QBE as illustrated earlier, it doesn't matter which way the data, and subsequently the stock, actually went — the short trade was a better trade than being long. If the data had been good, and say the stock had risen by 2 or 3 per cent, would the short trade have been a bad one? The answer is no — the expected return still favoured it. Unfortunately, because we don't see the failed potential outcomes, many traders wrongly believe that the final outcome was the best or the most likely and so they make all judgements based on the final outcome. As with Steven Bradbury at the Winter Olympics, though, the final outcome is not always the most likely or the one to back if we face the same situation again. While I realise that this idea can be hard for many traders to get around, it's important to do so.

Every day, the majority of traders are oblivious to the risks they are taking with their positions because they fail to conduct the type of analysis described in this chapter. Sometimes it doesn't matter and they make a profit despite (not because of) their analysis. On the occasions when they suffer large losses, for example with QBE, they will use the 'unforeseen event' defence. Some will even take comfort in the fact that so many others got caught too. We should not settle for either of these mindsets.

A note for automated and program traders: as a non-programmer I do not know how you go about programming in so many potential outcomes that have not occurred, or designing a system that reflects pricing in and market positioning. For example, share traders will need to include short-selling information and update this each day. As with manual traders, though, if your system does not incorporate this type of analysis then it's likely to be less robust.

When weighing up possible future moves we must include all possible outcomes. It's possible for a contract that has been rallying to rally further after data, but it will usually require very bullish data to push it further, or for the market to be in a strong bull- or bubble-type mode. In that way it's important not to create a rule-of-thumb short cut as a trading strategy but to trade the market as it is on that day.

Finally, while I have used share market examples in this chapter, the principle of pricing in and market positioning is valid across all markets. For markets such as bonds and currencies, the data that the market will be waiting for will tend to be macro-economic figures such as unemployment and inflation. Commodity markets have their important pieces of scheduled data too, and part of our due diligence process is to find out what data and news affects the markets we are trading and looking at.

Summary

- The assumption that markets are ahead is incorrect.
- Markets price in outcomes that may or may not be correct.
- Every day there is the possibility that markets find out if they are right, but data releases are scheduled occasions when this will certainly occur.
- We need to include pricing in and market positioning every day and with every trade.
- The magnitude of the move is at least equally as important as probability.
- This is an area where we can improve over time.

Chapter 9
Volatility

In this chapter ...

I explain the concept of volatility and show you how to integrate it into your trading. It's probably fair to say that everyone who is involved in the financial industry knows the term 'volatility', but how many actually understand the concept of volatility and how it affects markets and therefore profitability? I believe that among retail traders, their brokers and educators, there is a critical lack of knowledge of volatility and, in parts, there is misinformation on the topic.

I came across a perfect example of misinformation about volatility as I was planning this chapter. A broker was providing some of his 'advice' to retail investors. His first comment was that investors need volatility to make money; if you buy a stock, you need it to be volatile in order to generate a good profit. As I will explain, this suggestion shows a lack of knowledge about what volatility really is.

His second piece of advice was provided after he was asked how he works out what sort of range a stock might trade in over the future. He answered that a good rule of thumb to work out a stock's trading range for the year ahead was to use the square root of its share price. When I heard this, I nearly fell off my chair. It is laughable to suggest that completely different stocks that happen to have the same share price could be assessed with the same equation—with no individual input—in order to guess future volatility. There was no mention of terms such as 'historical volatility' or 'implied volatility'—terms that anyone with real options knowledge would use when discussing or analysing volatility and potential price ranges. I have traded derivatives since I was 18, for nearly 25 years, and I had never heard of this suggestion; views such as this had disappeared even before my career had started, as understanding of options and volatility had greatly evolved and improved.

Volatility is a topic that is generally viewed as being advanced, and is therefore omitted in many trading books and courses. However, when that happens misinformation fills the void, as we saw with the broker. We will undoubtedly experience the effects of both low and high volatility, and our profitability will be affected—so putting this subject in the 'too hard' basket is not an option. I have already explained how we will need to adapt our trading size according to volatility, so an understanding of volatility is actually essential to us. Again we will find that knowledge can provide better insights and edge over others.

Contrary to what the broker said, times of higher volatility will actually hurt most traders and investors, and they particularly hurt technical analysis traders. They will be further occasions of 'unforeseen' losses for most, often simply because their lack of knowledge means that they can't foresee what they don't know and can't look for.

At the start of the part II I write that one of the core principles to enjoying a sustainable trading career is being able to trade in as many different market conditions as possible. To this end, it's well worth taking the time to learn more about volatility, how it's measured and how to include volatility analysis in your trading. This will particularly help you to understand and trade through periods of higher volatility.

What is volatility?

There are actually four ways of discussing volatility:

- *Future volatility.* The $1 million question! Every trader wants to know, but of course it can only be known after the event. Traders try to gauge what it might be, using some of the other terms.

- *Forecast volatility.* This is someone's guesstimate of what future volatility will be. Various methods may be used, including looking at historical volatility.
- *Historical volatility.* This is the actual realised volatility of the underlying contract over a specific period of time. Historical volatility is often used to help predict future volatility; however, as with any approach that uses past information, we need to remember that the future may not (or is unlikely to) mirror the past.
- *Implied volatility.* This is a measure of the volatility that the options market implies will occur for the underlying contract. For example if the options on MSFT.US stock are trading on an implied volatility of 10 per cent, then they are implying that the underlying MSFT.US shares will have a range of +/− 10 per cent. The implied volatility figure is annualised with a probability of 67 per cent (one standard deviation) because the options pricing model assumes normal distribution (a bell-shaped curve).

The two most-used concepts are historical and implied volatility, so it's worth comparing them and providing some extra information; table 9.1 gives a breakdown.

Table 9.1: implied and historical volatility

Implied volatility	Historical volatility
Based on options prices	Based on the price of the underlying contract
Measures how much volatility the underlying contract will have in the future as measured by the price of its options	Measures how much the price of the underlying contract itself has varied over a specific period of time in the past
Instantaneous — is shown by current option prices	Lags
Forward looking	Backward looking

Using implied volatility requires applying options knowledge to our trading. This is not the first time I have advocated using options knowledge, but of all of the ideas that I have suggested, it should be well within the grasp of most traders. As with any new knowledge, it may require some time to sink in, and further time to incorporate properly, but there is no reason why we should not aim high and learn new skills and knowledge.

While most products have options derived from them, we will typically only be able to find reliable information on the options if they are listed and traded on an exchange. This will be the case for shares and futures. However, while currency options are heavily traded derivatives, they are over-the-counter (OTC) products, which means that, generally, retail traders will not get access to pricing and open interest information. So if you plan to trade currencies you may find it harder to find this type of information. Actually, this is an area where a good broker can add value, provided of course that they have good options knowledge.

Worryingly, there are even many private options traders who do not understand what implied volatility is, even though it's a core concept of options trading. Again we have the financial junk-food industry to thank for that, with their usual claims that it's possible to be profitable with limited knowledge. Many simplistic option courses omit concepts such implied volatility, because they fear they are too difficult for some retail traders to grasp.

There is no reason to fear the idea of implied volatility; it's quite simple to understand. If we input the price of any option into an option pricing model it will reflect a certain (implied) volatility for the underlying contract; this is the way that options traders try to guess what the future volatility will be. By looking at the implied volatility of an option we can see what the options market is pricing in for the near future of the underlying contract. If option prices (implied volatility) start to rise, then the traders are pricing in higher volatility and vice versa if they fall.

As an example, if JKL stock, trading at $2.00, has options available and we saw that these options were trading at an implied volatility of 15 per cent, then we would say that this is what the option market is pricing in to be the future volatility of JKL stock. If we apply the 15 per cent to the share price of $2.00 we would get a range of $1.70–$2.30, which is what the options market believes will be the range for the stock for the next 12 months, with a probability of 67 per cent (one standard deviation).

Many traders will use historical volatility as a basis for deciding what implied (or future) volatility should be. Good traders will know that they need to adapt or modify expectations, because historical volatility is what has happened in the past and of course the future is unlikely to mirror the past. Again, they will need to apply concepts such as pricing in and what could happen in the coming weeks and months in order for their analysis to be more forward-thinking. Historical volatility is often broken down into different time frames; for example, traders might examine 20-day historical volatility or 90-day historical volatility, depending on personal preferences and the time frame of their trading.

To return to the broker's volatility analysis mentioned at the start of the chapter (if only to dispel another myth) it should be clear that simply using the square root of a share price does not incorporate any of the concepts stated here. If we looked at two different shares that happened to have the same share price, the future range will be determined by volatility, not by the price. To suggest that the share price influences the volatility of any contract is nonsense.

As an example let's look at figure 9.1, a comparison chart of two Australian stocks, Telstra (TLS.AU) and FMG (FMG.AU). Please note the different price scales for each stock, TLS on the left and FMG on the right.

Figure 9.1: comparison chart of Telstra and FMG

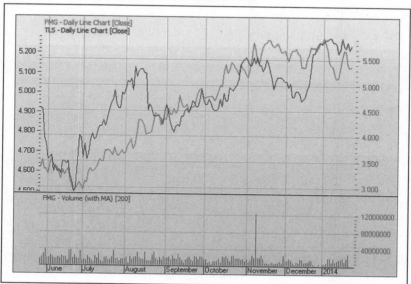

We first need to understand what these two contracts are; Telstra is a telecommunications provider, formerly state owned, and since privatisation it has become a staple for all portfolios in Australia, as it pays a high dividend. FMG is an iron ore–mining firm that has, like many mining firms, seen its fair share of highs and lows. It pays a small dividend but remains more of a growth stock, as opposed to Telstra, which is seen very much as a stable, yield play. So these are two very different types of shares.

You will see that at the time of this graph (late January 2014) both shares are trading at roughly the same price of around $5.25, but if we look back over the previous six months we will see a huge difference in trading range. Going forward, should we now believe that these two stocks will have similar future volatility simply because their share prices are now the same? The notion is absurd. Given the nature of the two companies and the two share prices, most knowledgeable traders and investors would continue to believe that FMG will be a higher volatility stock. The future range will be based on volatility, not on the share price itself. Table 9.2 provides further information from the day this chart was obtained:

Table 9.2: volatility of TLS and FMG

	20-day historical volatility	Implied volatility
TLS	9%	14.75%
FMG	27.8%	42.5%

Source: Data obtained from www.impliedvolatility.com.au.

The differences are stark and, while both options markets were implying higher volatility going forward than had been experienced recently, the expectations for FMG were significantly higher than for TLS. Whatever the final outcome, this is what I would expect knowledgeable traders to price in. If anyone were to offer FMG options at the same implied volatility as TLS options (which would suggest they have the same future volatility), then they would be the most popular person in the Australian options market — every option market-maker would fight to trade against that person. Despite the fact that both share prices are similar, the 20-day historical volatility (the realised volatility) was substantially different; one was 9 per cent, the other almost 28 per cent. There is no connection between the share price and the volatility of the contract.

Using historical and implied volatility in our trading

For the purposes of this book we need only investigate the basics of what implied volatility is and what it tells us. Historical volatility analysis is also interesting for us to understand. (Note that there can be some seasonality issues with both.) As we build up knowledge of our specialist area, we will gain a good understanding of typical levels of historical and implied volatility for the markets we follow.

As explained previously, we will use volatility analysis to judge position size; as volatility increases, or if we believe we will enter a period of higher volatility, then we will decrease our position size. Implied volatility is a good tool here because it is forward looking. If you note that implied volatility is significantly higher than historical volatility, then it suggests that options traders are expecting increased volatility going forward. This can therefore provide us with a good clue. Indeed if we look again at the TLS and FMG examples, we will see that for both contracts, the implied volatility is significantly higher than the historical figure. The timing is one of the critical issues here, with the figures being taken in mid January. The historical volatility covers the period of the holiday season and New Year, when markets were quieter. Going forward, options traders were envisaging higher volatility and more movement than was experienced during that holiday period, which would make sense as the market was closed for a number of days during that time. There was also some crucial data due out in the following few days that was potentially market moving. Note again the importance of being forward looking rather than simply basing decisions on the historical data.

We should also expect the possibility of increased volatility in the run up to and possibly after important data, and I have already discussed how we should lower position size if we hold trades over these periods.

As well as position sizing, our targets (and therefore stop loss levels) will be influenced by our volatility expectations. In times of higher volatility we might have a larger target, but of course our position size will be smaller—and vice versa for times of lower volatility. Times of lower volatility are typically trending markets, in which case there is usually less chance of our stop loss being activated and, as long as the trade is good and information remains the same, we will usually be resetting targets as the market grinds in our direction.

Therefore, as stated in chapter 7, both our position size and targets and stops will be influenced by our expectations of volatility. Volatility will affect our trading, so it seems obvious to me that we should incorporate it into our analysis and decision making, remembering that we are trying to weigh up future expectations. We do also need to take into account the volumes and liquidity of the options we are looking at and pay less attention if volumes are very small. As long as liquidity is good, though, options traders provide us with another set of participants from which we can take information.

Trading in times of high volatility

The reality is that during times of high volatility, many (if not most) traders and investors get thrown around like a sock in the washing machine. Not only do they tend to lose money, but the psychological roller-coaster that they ride leaves them mentally exhausted too. As part of our desire to trade in as many market conditions as possible, we should try to develop ways to trade in times of higher volatility.

For reasons unknown to me (and surely not related to me) I have had the dubious pleasure of trading through some of the worst market crashes and periods of highest volatility over the past 25 years, in many different markets. It seemed that whichever market I started to trade, no matter how placid it had been, would suddenly take on a new, more volatile complexion. So I have had to develop and use techniques to cope with periods of high volatility.

I have already explained the need to reduce position size and amend targets accordingly, and it should go without saying now that we must cut losses as soon as our information or stop loss tells us to. In addition we will need to reduce the time frame in which we are trading; trying to judge even a week ahead during times of volatility is too difficult. Indeed, even keeping an overnight position can be tough. If you look back at previous times of high volatility, for example during the various euro crises a few years ago, completely different news and data would hit the markets almost daily. Almost any trade had the potential to be stopped out. While many traders believe that in these times they should widen stop loss levels to avoid being stopped out, I find it hard to believe that they can be certain enough in their analysis to do so. High volatility means that no-one really knows what is going on—anyone who believes they know better is likely to be overconfident.

For those who are trading with their own capital, I suggest it's preferable to reduce the time frame to the shortest possible and trade intra-day during times of high volatility, avoiding holding even overnight positions, as the information on our watchlists will be constantly changing. Luckily, high volatility provides many opportunities to generate profits intra-day while finishing the day without a position. Then it doesn't matter what happens overnight; we come in the next day and do it all over again. In fact, most professional traders that I know prefer to trade this way every day, and I explain it in more depth in chapter 10.

Options also provide us with other ways to trade during periods of high volatility. They enable us to construct positions that have less exposure to market direction but still have great risk/reward profiles. For example, holding a long position in a particular stock, or say gold futures, may become too difficult during a time of high volatility—but we can replace the trade with an out-of-the-money long call or long call spread position that requires less capital, has a defined risk and excellent reward potential. Usually it's easier to hold these types of options trades through periods of high volatility and, in fact, the high volatility should add extra profit to the option trade. Once again, knowledge, on this occasion of options, will increase our ability to construct the right trade for the right market conditions and improve our profitability.

What does high volatility look like?

The broker quoted at the start of this chapter stated that investors need volatility to make money. He was inferring that when you buy a stock you need the market to move a long way in order to make a lot of money; isn't that volatility? The answer depends on how the move occurs and in what time frame. If the stock doubles in one day then yes, that is volatile. However, if it moves higher over a period of say six months, then that will not be volatility at work; it's a trend. Trends and volatility are almost complete opposites.

We sometimes explain how to recognise volatility on a chart by imagining you had a piece of string that you laid over the chart. If you had to wind the string up and down over all of the moves, then the higher the volatility, the more string is needed. A trend will use up far less string than a contract that has moved up and down.

If we look again at FMG stock in figure 9.2, we can see this in action. Note that the share price scale is on the right and the volatility scale on the left.

Figure 9.2: FMG volatility

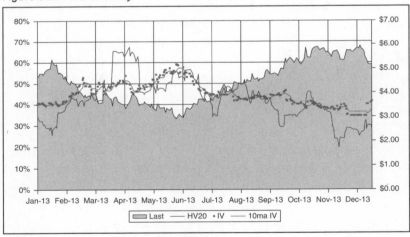

Source: Chart courtesy of www.impliedvolatility.com.au.

If we first examine the period from the share price low in June 2013 up to the middle of November 2013 we will see that FMG's share price almost doubles from below $3.00 to $5.75. While this is a significant move in dollar terms, we can see that the realised, historical volatility (HV20) over that period fell from around 54 per cent to less than 20 per cent at the mid–November share-price high.

It's not the size of the move, necessarily; it is the way it moves and length of time the move takes that determines if it's a period of high volatility. Here, a rise over several months means that we had a slow trend and investors were rewarded for low volatility.

Then, we can see that the historical volatility starts to rise even before the move downwards at the end of the graph as the two-way market swings replace the upward trend (perhaps better seen in figure 9.3). The two-way movement that many traders would see as sideways movement from late November onwards is actually a period of rising volatility—the opposite of a trend. This rising volatility has not helped investors, as suggested by our broker; it's probably causing them some anguish over what to do.

Figure 9.3: FMG daily chart

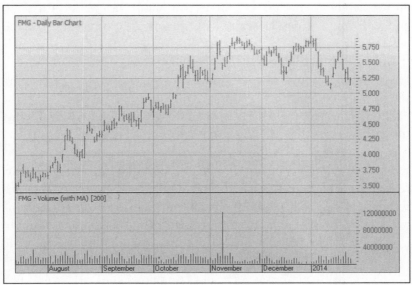

Figure 9.3 also helps to dispel the myth of the relationship between the square root of a share price and its volatility. For example, during the period between February and August 2013, FMG shares often trade around a price of $3.50; yet the realised historical volatility during those periods varies greatly. On one occasion it's around 45 per cent; on another, it's 62 per cent; and on yet another it's 35 per cent. Future trading ranges are also very different.

Many markets exhibit rising volatility when they fall, and falling volatility when they rise; these tend to be the markets where most participants trade from the long side, including share and bond markets. The reasons are quite straightforward, in that falling prices for these markets typically mean losses for most involved, and losses will lead to some degree of panic, poor decision making, and so on. Rising prices, though, suit most participants, and so the moves can be more orderly, as we see with FMG.

So if we're trading shares and we expect a steep fall, then we should also factor in the possibility, or even the probability, of rising volatility, and vice versa if we expect a rally. For markets such as currencies and commodities, the relationship is not always the same and will often depend on the way traders are positioned and the scale of the move.

For our trading, now that we know what volatility is, we can adapt our techniques, analysis, position sizing and targets accordingly when we see volatility change. Knowing that options' implied volatility tries to be forward looking, we can sometimes get clues to future movement by looking at what options traders are pricing in.

Of course, as we're looking at pricing in again, we should remember that all is not always straightforward. For example, remembering that the markets move the most when traders are wrongly positioned, it's also interesting for us to know what options traders are thinking, in case they are wrong. This is particularly important when they are pricing in low volatility going forward, typically after a recent period of low volatility.

You may have heard references to the VIX Index, which is a volatility index constructed using options data. As with all markets, there are always traders who look backward for their analysis, and so there are times when many traders are making decisions based on historical data alone. So, during periods of low volatility, we can often see the VIX Index trade at low levels. When the VIX is low (and this applies to all options' implied volatility) it tells us two things. First, that traders are expecting low future volatility and therefore, second, they are positioned for that occurrence. This means that any jump in volatility will be unexpected to both traders of the underlying contract and traders of the derivatives (options).

So we should use rising implied volatility as a warning that some traders see higher volatility ahead; this is all part of looking for disconfirmation and information across a wide variety of different markets. But we should not be afraid to trade against the implied volatility expectations if our information suggests doing so. Sometimes implied volatility rises before a move, sometimes it doesn't; as we have seen, trading is rarely clear-cut. Instead, it usually involves the collection and dissemination of various pieces of information. I have seen many traders try to construct simple rules using the VIX, such as 'when the VIX is low, volatility is low and share markets rise', but such rules are far too simplistic. We always need to trade in the 'now', rather than by historical rules of thumb.

I hope that this introduction to volatility has not been too difficult to grasp. While this is often seen as a more advanced topic, the reality is that it will affect everyone's trading, whether you're a newbie or an experienced trader, so we may as well all try to understand it from the start. If you put the topic of volatility into the 'too hard' basket then your trading will be the worse for it; we cannot simply decide to ignore topics that look too hard. Again, it will take time to understand this area to a level where you are confident applying it, and you should also expect to improve with experience. We see again how knowledge can provide edge both in terms of analysis and in trade selection. The more knowledge we have, the better our understanding of what is happening and of finding the right trade for the right market. I'm a strong believer that correctly applying a good knowledge of options will greatly assist our trading, and this is an area that all traders should learn more about. (Just be wary of the junk-food industry courses that typically just involve selling options to generate income — until the inevitable large losses hit.)

Summary

- Volatility will affect your profitability, so you need to learn about it.
- Historical volatility is realised volatility; implied volatility is forward looking.
- Adapt your trading according to volatility expectations; for example, shorten the time frame and reduce trading size in periods of increased volatility.
- Options can be very useful tools, both in analysing volatility and constructing positions.

Chapter 10
Become the bookmaker: how the pros trade

In this chapter...

I want to bring together the techniques that I have previously examined and show you a style of trading that is favoured by most of the successful professional traders that I have known. While I have shown different ways to approach trading, the methods that I explain in this chapter encompass nearly all of the techniques and suggestions that I have described. They reflect a professional approach to trading, where the trader views himself as a price-maker and a central cog in the market, rather than a price-taker who is constantly battling against the market. So, rather than trade against the market we become the market. As the saying goes, 'if you can't beat them, join them'.

Over the past nine chapters we have explored a number of different topics that all have an important role to play if we are to enjoy sustainable trading profits. Sustainable, successful trading requires a good knowledge base adapted to an understanding of how markets really work, backed up by good discipline. There are no easy paths to success, but there are plenty of short cuts to failure. Good professional traders don't become so overnight; they improve over time as their knowledge and range of techniques increases.

The techniques and suggestions in this book are based on nearly 25 years of experience trading alongside hundreds of traders. I have seen good traders first hand, and I have also witnessed others lose their trading account in less than a day; typically I have learned more from the failures than successes, and much of this book is based on avoiding the mistakes of those who have failed.

Many, if not most, of the trading books and courses on offer are based on the philosophy of 'Follow me; I've made lots of money', but I do not subscribe to that approach; you may be following someone who has taken lots of risk, or whose success was the result of random rewards. In my opinion, an element of learning from others' failures is essential in any analysis of trading techniques.

It's very hard to beat the markets day after day, year after year; it's hard to consistently predict where the market might go days or weeks ahead. Those who claim they have found ways to do this through charts or past data are typically part of the financial junk-food industry—they are telling you what you want to hear. So the real professionals choose a different approach based on playing a different role in the market; I call this becoming the bookmaker rather than the punter.

Be the bookmaker

The horse racing industry has many similarities to trading; every day people are betting they can beat the market and make money;

many use 'systems' or tips that they believe give them edge, but in reality they are relying on noise. There are numerous books explaining how to become a profitable punter; meanwhile, most punters lose. Yet there is a small group who generally make money each and every day. They do not try to predict race results; rather, they position themselves according to the market flows and they aim to profit from the flow of money in the system and the fact that most punters don't mind giving up edge every time they trade.

I am, of course, talking about the bookmakers. Yet despite their continued and sustained success you rarely see books or courses offering to teach you how to be a bookmaker—most people still want to become punters even though the success rate for them is low. Perhaps people think that the bookmaker's role is less glamorous or perhaps even boring, or maybe they wrongly believe that there are more successful punters than there really are. But the name of the game is to make money consistently and enjoy a long career making money; surely we should embrace whatever techniques will provide the best potential long-term return.

The market's equivalent of bookmakers are market-makers; traders who specialise in one contract and act as price setters for that contract, trading in and out of others traders' business. In the days of floor (pit) trading, traders would pay sometimes significant sums for the right to be a market-maker (called a 'local') on the floor. In return they would have access to low commission rates, usually some rebates from the exchange (because they were high-volume traders) and, importantly, they would have the ability to be price-makers, thereby being able to set the bid and offer the prices at which they wanted to buy and sell.

This picture is my badge from when I was an options market-maker (local) on the London International Financial Futures Exchange (LIFFE) back in the 1990s (and it was a really bad hair day!). Each trader had a three letter mnemonic that was used instead of real names whenever we traded. The white circle showed that I was registered and permitted to trade options, while the shaded area around the white circle showed that I was a local (someone who traded with their own capital or that of a private backer, rather than a bank) and that I would receive rebates from the exchange for scratch trades (trades where we buy and sell for the same price, which was common as a market-maker).

Flow trading

When floor-traded markets such as futures and shares became computer-based, they also changed from being market-maker–led to being order-driven; no longer were there dedicated market-makers. Instead, orders were put into the system and matched accordingly. Initially it was thought that the role of market-makers in these products was finished, but instead there has remained a niche, particularly in futures markets, for those with the right skills to trade in and out of the order flow (known as scalping or flow trading). In particular for futures trading, new specialist platforms have been created specifically for flow traders, and many brokers specialise in providing low commission rates for the high-volume flow traders. While you may not read much about these types of traders, there remain hundreds if not thousands of them all over the world—but predominantly in cities and countries that used to house the futures exchanges, such as Chicago, London and Singapore.

Flow traders continue to specialise by trading one market. Most use futures because they offer a number of advantages over other products. These include a transparent order book; the ability to set the spread, and trade inside the spread (that is, the ability to trade on any price we wish); specialist platforms and brokers; special margin rates for intra-day traders, meaning that only a small account size can provide the opportunity for excellent returns; limited counterparty risk, as trades are matched by the exchanges; and everyone in the world essentially sees the same information. (In the appendix I lay out the pros and cons of various products, and that you will see that futures still offer flow traders the best opportunity.)

There is a range of different futures markets, with different ranges of volatility and liquidity, and in different time zones. Flow traders will select the market that they believe suits their personality best, but most prefer to trade very liquid, less volatile contracts. As with the techniques that I explain in chapter 5, I prefer to trade a contract where I can gather information from both positively and negatively correlated markets to aid my decision making.

I cannot explain all of the techniques and strategies of flow traders in a book, as there is a degree of complexity to it that is impossible to explain in print. However, the essence of flow trading is to take very short-term trades (often a few seconds) using the bid and offer spread to our advantage, and trading in and out of the flow of business in our market. We can profit from other traders' market orders through using the bid/offer spread, as these are not always executed at the best price. We can also pick off stop loss orders and some limit orders if and when the market conditions change. Flow traders, like all market professionals, understand the power and profitability of using the bid/offer spread correctly, as explained in chapter 1.

We look to make small amounts on each trade, say $20 to $30, but do so dozens of times a day, thereby potentially generating decent profits of hundreds if not thousands of dollars per day. These are the profits that most traders don't care about; most are trading on a longer time frame and so they think nothing of giving away $20 for the spread. But those with low commissions can profit from these small amounts that others don't want.

At the end of our trading day we will have no position, so we don't care what happens overnight; this greatly helps us to enjoy a long-term career because we are not always predicting where the market will go, and we have no overnight market direction risk. Account sizes can be as little as $5000 or $10 000 with an intra-day margin per contract of as little as $1000 or less, meaning that a good flow trader can generate excellent returns on their capital. However, as with all trading, only those with the right skills, knowledge and discipline will succeed.

Good flow traders have a very high percentage of winning trades; I aim for over 80 per cent winners, around 15 per cent scratch trades (that is, buying and selling for the same price) and around 5 per cent losers. It should be noted that these types of figures are for experienced flow traders. Some flow traders who trade the very low volatility contracts do work to a lower percentage of profitable trades, but the key is that they will look to scratch trades rather than lose. This is another vital point to flow trading: replacing losing trades with scratch trades can greatly help profitability; professional futures traders have understood this for many years.

Elements for flow-trading success

A few elements are crucial for success. First, losses must be cut quickly; we cannot afford to hold losses, so great discipline is required. The speed of trades means that quick responses are required; this will not suit everyone. Very low commissions are a prerequisite, so a specialist broker is required. It's essential that commissions for a round trip (both sides of the trade combined) are lower than the tick size for the contract you are trading.

Flow trading can be a very intense form of trading; we spend hours staring at our screen, and when business picks up we can make multiple trades in a short space of time. There can be periods of relative calm and few opportunities followed by bursts of activity, so patience is required too. All this means that flow trading will not suit everyone.

Flow trading is a professional style of trading, so it's likely that new traders may struggle. We still use the watchlist information to find clues about possible direction, but we do so on a much shorter time scale. In reality, the skills and techniques that flow traders use are the same as I have outlined in this book; it's just that they are applied in a much faster time frame. Therefore, to become a successful flow trader, the use of watchlists, and so on, will need to become second nature.

Flow traders also track changes to the order book and incorporate this information into their trading. Information could be an increase in the bids or a sudden disappearance of many offers. There is a lot of information in a contract's order book for those who learn how to read them, so if you are trading a market that does not provide access to an order book (for example, currencies) you will be missing some crucial information.

Flow traders need to trade in the 'now'; by that I mean there is no time for conservativeness or overanalysing what happened yesterday or even an hour ago. Flow traders will only be profitable if they obtain and apply a good knowledge of how their market works; there is no time for false beliefs or assumptions, no place for rule of thumb patterns and indicators. We must trade what is really happening now. We need to be able to switch between long and short positions instantly as the information changes—again, a must for all good traders.

All this means that flow trading encompasses the true essence of trading—to trade the markets as they are, not our views of them. An added bonus is that we get instant feedback on our decisions and, as Thaler and Sunstein state in *Nudge*, we learn better if we get instant feedback on our decisions.

Flow trading's benefits

There are many benefits to flow trading for those who trade with their own money. First, only a small amount of capital is required to start off with. Second, the capital being risked per trade is very small; typically we might risk only $20 per trade. Even if a flow trader had a string of five losses in a row, the loss may only amount to $100 or so. Finishing each day with no position is also an advantage, as explained already; our chances of enjoying a long career will be enhanced if we have no overnight direction risk.

Flow trading is also a great form of trading during times of high volatility. I explain in chapter 9 how, during times of high volatility, we should reduce our trading time frame—and flow trading does just that. It can also be possible to profit from the panic of many other traders during these times, as their market orders can provide great edge to specialists who use the bid/offer spread. This last point is just one way that specialists gain edge, and flow traders should profit from their specialisation. Good flow traders see steady, daily profits with limited scope for a big losing day; they therefore get off the trading roller-coaster and instead enjoy the compounded profits that I have suggested is a better scenario to aim for.

I also like the fact that we make lots of trades (I have traded over 100 times a day during busy days) because this will lead to us being desensitised to trading. Too many private traders become too emotional when they trade. They are often filled with excitement and/or apprehension when they trade, and this will affect their decision making. Rather like a golfer practising so many four-foot putts that they become routine, or a football player practising endless numbers of penalty kicks, by trading many times a day we become less emotional about our trades. When you have completed thousands of trades, each trade is less exciting, which is how it should be—we don't want to trade for excitement. We only want to trade for success. Those who get caught up in the excitement are usually gamblers, whereas professionals only enter the business to win. Trading for small profits and losses also helps to remove the thrill of the trade.

It may well be that flow trading is not for you, and I certainly wouldn't expect all retail traders to want to use this approach. However,

I wanted to explain the techniques that many professional traders use and why they use them. If we examine the ideas that I have laid out in this book in table 10.1, we can see how flow trading fits them.

Table 10.1: flow trading and my trading principles

Discipline/principle	Flow trading
Preserve capital	Yes
Trade in all market conditions	Yes
Understand context	Yes
Employ 'System 2'	Yes, to a degree
Short time frame	Yes
Use bid/offer spread to our advantage	Yes
Specialise	Yes
Steady profits rather than roller-coaster	Yes
Small losses only	Yes
No overnight direction risk	Yes
Trading differently to most retail traders (who usually lose)	Yes
Requires business-minded approach	Yes, decisions such as platforms and fees are crucial
Requires professional-level knowledge	Yes
Requires independent thinking	Yes
Eliminates random rewards	Yes, by aiming for a high success rate we should be rewarded regularly, not randomly

Around the world there are firms who teach and employ flow traders, who have dozens of traders in a trading room all trading in a similar way in different markets. I know of no trading rooms anywhere that have dozens of successful traders using chart patterns, candlesticks or other methods of the financial junk-food industry. There is a failure rate of flow traders, but I think it's fair to say that the percentage of successful futures flow traders is quite significantly higher than the overall percentage of successful futures traders.

Unlike bank and hedge-fund traders, private traders usually don't have access to ongoing sources of capital, nor do they have risk managers or senior traders to refer to. Hence my belief that it's preferable for them to avoid trying to predict markets and instead focus on making smaller intra-day profits and avoiding overnight risk.

Some have suggested that the increasing number of automated traders has rendered flow traders redundant, but I don't subscribe to that view. Some markets have become more difficult to trade, but there remains a niche, especially during more volatile days when many automated traders sit out. It's also wrong to believe that most automated traders are successful. Some are good, others not, as they employ similar methods to technical traders, so the latter can be still be a source of profits for flow traders.

If need be, flow trading can be accompanied and complemented by some medium-term positions on the occasions when you might want to express a view or take advantage of market positioning. This should be done according to the techniques outlined in the previous chapters, and I typically use options for this.

Summary

- Flow trading has many psychological benefits for traders.
- Trade in and out of the market's business rather than taking on the market.
- Use the bid/offer spread to your advantage.
- Flow trading requires relatively small account sizes and generates relatively small profits and losses.
- Flow trading requires concentration, discipline and quick responses, so it may not suit everyone.

CONCLUSION

My aim with this book is twofold: to expose how the financial junk-food industry operates, and to explain the knowledge, techniques and mindset that are required of successful traders. As I stated at the start of the book, I don't believe that everyone can be a successful trader—but that doesn't mean we shouldn't try. The important thing is to not put too much capital at risk during the learning process. There can be good rewards from trading over the long term but, of course, you need to make it to the long term—which means the ability to get through each day and week in the short term.

Unfortunately it's very likely that much of what you have previously read or heard about trading has come from either the sell side or the financial junk-food industry or both. That is predominantly because these groups are better at selling themselves. Survivorship bias means that we don't get to see the many traders who have quit the business or lost substantial amounts of money as a result of the junk-food brigade; you only get to see the few glowing testimonials that may or may not be real.

So I sincerely hope that the early chapters helped to show where you may be going wrong and/or why your existing beliefs and techniques may not be as reliable as you were told. Before we are able to move on we first need to understand what we are doing wrong.

The meat of the book has dealt with explaining the tools needed to build a sustainable trading career. Over time the knowledge and techniques that I have explained will hopefully become second nature, but don't expect this to occur overnight. We should all seek to continually improve and to remember that there is always more to learn. Trading is a complex business because each situation we face is different; that's why understanding and incorporating context into our trading is so vital.

It's common for traders to be told that we can employ the same technique or indicator every time the market looks the same, but this is both misleading and likely to be an unreliable short cut. If you base your trading decisions on charts, then the markets often do look the same—but this is not because they *are* the same, but rather because the method of analysis you are using (the chart) omits significant amounts of context. If I look at the world through blue-tinted spectacles, then the world will always look blue—but that doesn't mean it *is* blue. In this way, the (mis)use of charts is one of the biggest issues that confronts would-be traders. Charts have their uses, but they are limited; they look back and don't contain enough information for us to look forward.

I have introduced concepts such as pricing in and volatility, which are usually viewed as too complex, but I believe they are essential to good trading. There is no science to working out what is being priced in; it's part of the skill of a good trader, and I would advise against developing a rule of thumb strategy to deal with it.

Remember at all times that if you are unsure what to do, DO NOTHING. You can always watch what happens and observe how your trade would have fared.

I ended by discussing flow trading, a style of short-term trading that is employed by hundreds (if not thousands) of professional traders around the world. It will not suit everyone but does have a number of advantages for retail traders.

I sincerely hope that you have enjoyed the book and that your trading improves as a result. Hopefully the financial junk-food industry has lost another potential victim!

Best regards,

Gary

APPENDIX

Table A1 shows the characteristics of various products evaluated from the perspective of a private trader who wishes to trade intra-day as I describe in chapter 10. Each criterion has been rated between 0 and 3 ticks. I have omitted CFDs for a few reasons. First, they are not available in all countries. Second, they can differ from provider to provider, so it is harder to summarise. In general I am not a fan of market–maker CFDs because you are trading against the market-maker as well as the market and usually cannot set the price. Direct market access (DMA) CFDs can offer some opportunities but it depends on the provider.

Table A1: the characteristics of various products for intra-day trading

	Futures	Shares	FX
Orders in the order book visible	✓✓✓	✓✓✓	
Transparent trading price and volume	✓✓✓	✓✓✓	
Ability to set the price, buy on the bid (sell on offer) and trade inside the spread	✓✓✓	✓✓✓	✓
24-hour trading	✓✓		✓✓✓
Same market information for all participants	✓✓✓	✓✓✓	

(continued)

Table A1: the characteristics of various products for intra-day trading *(cont'd)*

	Futures	Shares	FX
Reduced counterparty/ broker risk	✓✓	✓✓	
Exchange traded	✓✓✓	✓✓✓	
Specialist independent (of broker) platforms	✓✓✓	✓	✓
Specialist brokers for active traders	✓✓✓	✓✓	✓✓✓
Transparent derivatives available to increase trade ideas and provide further information	✓✓✓	✓✓✓	
Ability to trade long and short with equal ease	✓✓✓	✓	✓✓✓
Ease of trading on margin or using leverage	✓✓✓	✓	✓✓✓
Low fees	✓✓✓	✓✓	✓✓✓
Intra-day tradeability	✓✓✓	✓	✓✓
Short term (a few days) tradeability	✓	✓✓✓	✓✓

I admit that there is a degree of subjectivity to this table; over time, as platforms and brokers evolve, the scores are likely to change.

Perhaps the relatively low score for FX will be the most controversial aspect of the table, so I will explain the reasons. I place great store by transparency of prices and the ability of all traders to play on a level field. In my opinion, retail FX traders are at a significant disadvantage to market professionals both in terms of the prices and activity that they see. Retail FX traders can only see the price activity that their provider shows, which will be a fraction of what is actually happening.

Compare this situation to futures: whether I am trading futures for a bank or for myself, the prices, order book and volumes that I see are the same as for someone trading from home. This is the significant benefit that trading an exchange–traded product provides for us.

In addition, many FX providers do not allow traders to trade inside the spread—clients must be price-takers, and again this is a huge disadvantage to active traders.

Of course, currency futures are available but currently they are not as liquid and as representative as they will perhaps become. Going forward, I believe that moving to a more open, transparent, exchange-traded structure will help retail FX traders.

As I have explained, the small amounts of edge that are given up by lack of transparency in pricing, trading on the wrong side of the spread and not seeing the current trading price all add up and diminish, or even eliminate, other edge we might have. Do not underestimate these issues, particularly if you want to trade intra-day. The longer you hold a position the less these issues will affect you, but of course then you will face other risks.

I realise that FX trading is the current flavour of the month and is being pushed hard by the industry, but sometimes you have to wonder why is it being pushed so hard and who is really profiting. Now you are aware of the financial junk-food industry you should be more wary of the overt sales pitches.

So for intra-day trading such as flow trading, futures have significant benefits over the other products and would be my product of choice.

Trading FX would require positions to be held for longer periods, but be aware of leverage risks. My view is that the current FX offering for retail traders is not quite what it could and should be and hopefully over time there will be changes and new developments that will help to level the playing field.

Shares are transparent products but can be difficult to trade intra-day due to smaller moves and higher costs relative to spread size. One of the key issues for intra-day traders is to ensure that the commissions per trade are smaller than the minimum spread size so that every trade, no matter how small the edge, will be profitable after commissions.

INDEX

analysis 3, 6, 7, 8, 19, 27, 31, 35,
39, 40, 49–50, 52, 53, 55, 61,
62, 63, 70, 73, 77, 79, 82, 85,
95–97, 109, 110, 118, 120–123,
124, 127, 129–130, 132, 138,
140, 141, 142, 143–144, 145,
147, 148, 152–153, 154–156,
158, 165, 167, 168, 169, 172,
173, 176; *see also* analysts;
information; position sizing and
management; watchlists
—fundamental 19, 78, 93–94,
157
—technical 9, 12, 15–17, 19,
22, 24, 25, 28, 36, 44, 45–46,
51, 54, 71, 76, 78, 93–94, 107,
124, 125–126, 127, 129, 137,
141, 143, 150–151, 162, 186
analysts 4–5, 7, 10, 20, 27, 45, 58,
72, 76, 77, 80, 86, 106, 148,
149, 150, 152; *see also* brokers;
sell side
—fundamental 10, 19, 141,
157
—technical 9, 10, 12, 25, 61, 63,
76, 124, 144, 156, 157
—vs traders 3–7

anchoring bias 27–38
automated trading strategies 140,
158, 184
availability bias 26–27

backtesting 49, 51, 86, 104, 134,
139, 150, 151, 153–154
banks and bank traders 3–4, 12, 18,
55, 60, 61, 69, 73, 74, 86, 89, 126,
178, 183; *see also* central banks;
hedge funds; professional traders
—investment 4, 10, 12, 13, 14,
18, 21, 58, 59, 102, 109, 122,
126, 156, 140
bear markets and bearish sentiment
54, 61, 67, 78, 94, 148, 152, 156
behavioural finance 11, 16–17,
23–24; *see also* Kahneman, Daniel
biases 24–36; *see also* heuristics;
weaknesses of traders
—in action 34–36
—anchoring 27–38
—availability 26–27
—confirmation 30–31, 35,
80–81
—conservativeness 28–29, 30,
35, 81

biases 24–36; *see also* heuristics;
  weaknesses of traders *(cont'd)*
  —hindsight 29–30, 81–82
  —overconfidence 28, 29
  —overcoming 37, 80–82, 97–98
  —overoptimism 29, 59, 78
  —representativeness 24–26
  —self-attribution 26, 29, 35, 45
  —status quo 32, 35
bid/ask spread 21–22
bid/offer spread 121, 183, 184
blame 29, 43, 45; *see also* bias,
  self-attribution
bookmaker, trading as 83, 176–178;
  see also market makers
brokers 63, 90, 91, 112; *see also* sell
  side
  —advice 5, 34–26, 161–162,
    165
  —choice of 100–104
  —commissions 102–103
  —customer support 103–104
  —platforms 100–101, 102, 105
  —role of 4–5, 6, 7, 9
  —safety of funds 103–104
  —services 105–106, 111, 114
  —vs traders 3–7
bubbles 60, 118, 155–156, 158
bull markets and bullish sentiment
  12, 40–41, 44, 54, 66, 76, 77,
  79, 81, 84, 85, 92, 118, 119, 144,
  149, 156, 158
business, trading as a; *see also*
  trading; trading capital
  —advice 100–104, 113
  —costs 101, 104–107, 112–113,
    114
  —decisions in trading 99–115;
    see also decision making
  —growth 107–108
  —Plan B 111–113

—re-evaluation 114
—requirements for 104–107
—tax advice 113
buy side 4, 6–7, 21–22; *see also* sell
  side

capital, trading *see* trading capital
central banks 19, 63, 64, 82, 97
CDSs (credit default swaps) 64–65,
  91, 93
CFDs (contracts for difference) 21,
  62, 68, 100, 101–102, 106, 119,
  102
charting packages 106–107
charts, using 12, 17, 30, 82, 86, 106,
  143, 144, 149, 151, 153, 170,
  176, 186
cognitive dissonance 31–34, 35,
  130
commissions 5, 6, 100, 101,
  102–103, 104, 114, 131, 133,
  177, 179, 180–181, 189
commodities 12, 59, 65, 72, 78, 90,
  92, 93, 100, 159, 172
company information 19–20, 34–
  35, 146, 149–150, 152, 157, 167
computers in trading business
  104–105, 111
confirmation bias 30–31, 35, 80–81
conservativeness bias 28–29, 30,
  35, 81
context, in decision making 27, 43,
  51, 58, 74, 81–82, 92–93, 94, 96,
  98, 138, 144, 148, 155, 183, 186;
  see also market(s)
  —ignoring 54–55
  —understanding markets 36,
    58, 59, 78, 85–87, 88, 98, 109,
    127, 132
contrarian views and trades 36, 44,
  69, 80, 146, 152, 155

convertible bonds 3–4
currency markets *see* markets, foreign exchange

data *see* information
decision making, trader 11, 20, 33, 40, 42, 140, 142–144; *see also* System 2
—facing up to poor 31–34, 35–36
—improving 35–36, 45–46, 56
derivatives 66–69, 85, 94, 112, 145, 162, 164, 173, 188, 189
discipline 32–33, 110, 118, 119, 137–138, 140, 175
disconfirmation 95–96, 147
Disposition Effect 32

Eastman Kodak 12
Efficient Market Hypothesis 71
Enron 12
entry and exit points *see* price
equity markets *see* markets, share
exchange traded products 101–102
exuberance 44, 59, 62, 79

finance industry *see* analysts; banks; brokers; central banks; hedge funds; managed funds; sell side
financial junk food industry 1, 15, 19, 22, 23, 39, 57, 108, 110, 117, 137, 142, 173, 183
—participants 3–9
flaws and weaknesses of traders 23–27, 137; *see also* biases
flow trading 178–184
—benefits of 182–84
FMG 165–166, 167, 170–172
forecasting 20, 26, 76, 148, 157, 163
—unreliability of long-term 10–11, 25–26, 27–28, 36, 86

foreign exchange (FX) 18, 21, 26–27, 59, 62–63, 73–74, 78, 81, 84, 87, 100, 101, 102, 106, 119, 144, 159, 164, 166, 187
fund managers 6, 10, 60, 73, 77, 118; *see also* finance industry; hedge funds; professional investors
futures 10, 11, 16, 59, 62, 63, 65, 66, 68, 74, 84, 87, 90, 92, 94, 100, 101, 102, 103, 105, 106–107, 108, 119, 129, 144, 164, 169, 178, 179, 180, 183
FX *see* foreign exchange

gambling 32, 34, 42, 48, 135, 182; *see also* bookmaker, trading as
Gann theory 16
gold 10, 68, 82, 83, 84, 91, 92, 93, 127–128, 169
greed and fear 23

hedge funds 4, 6, 13, 55, 60, 61, 63, 70, 83, 102, 109, 122, 126, 140, 183; *see also* banks; professional traders
hedging technique 63, 67–69, 80, 94, 97, 134
heuristics 16–17, 24–36, 58, 129; *see also* biases
hindsight bias 29–30, 81–82
humility 36, 132

Iluka 151–153
independent thinking, importance of 43–45
indicators 17–19
information *see also* knowledge; market(s); watchlists
—availability bias 26–27
—company 19–20, 34–35, 146, 149–150, 152, 157, 167

information *see also* knowledge;
   market(s); watchlists *(cont'd)*
—due 145–146
—economic 19–20, 72
—effect on markets 71–72
—following several markets
   78–80
—gathering 75, 93–94, 114
—good 27–28
—importance of 19–20, 153
—limited 26–28
—new 28, 31, 35
—news 91, 93, 93, 105–106,
   148, 146, 147, 167
—news feeds 105–106
—release of data 71–72
—using 26–27, 82–83
—vs noise 35, 75–77, 78
insider trading 142
internet providers 105, 111
internet trading forums/chat
   rooms 30–31, 44–45
investment banks *see* banks,
   investment; professional traders

Japanese stock market crash 33,
   118, 130
judgement 11, 24, 25, 26, 59, 64,
   71, 76, 79, 121, 122, 123, 125,
   127, 138, 158; *see also* decision
   making

Kahneman, Daniel 9, 16, 17, 24,
   25, 27, 26, 30, 36–37; *see also*
   behavioural finance
Keynes, John Maynard 28, 31, 32,
   36, 142
knowledge, need for 4, 5, 18,
   19–20, 22, 23, 27, 30, 40, 54,
   56, 57–74, 77, 78, 89, 93, 94,
   96, 97, 109, 113, 127, 128, 129,

138, 139, 140, 143–144, 145,
   150, 156, 161, 162, 163–164,
   166, 167, 169, 173, 175, 176,
   180, 181, 183; *see also* context;
   information; markets; watchlists

lateral thinking 96–97
leverage 6, 68, 101, 107, 119–120,
   128, 188, 189
lifestyle and trading 41–43
liquidity 13, 55, 62, 67, 102, 168,
   179
long side (buying shares) trading 5,
   59, 63, 69, 70, 78, 79, 145, 172
loss aversion 32, 146
losses 10, 18, 48, 51, 66, 80, 83, 135,
   146, 150, 154, 155, 172, 173,
   182, 183; *see also* biases; trading
   capital, preserving; stop loss;
   weaknesses and faults, trader
—avoiding 31–32, 46–49, 112, 125
—coping with 43–44
—cutting quickly 24, 37, 107,
   113, 118–119, 120, 129–130,
   134, 136, 137, 138, 169, 180
—facing up to 29, 32–34, 35,
   37, 41–42, 43–44, 45, 48, 51,
   158, 162
—not until you sell 35
—and risk 32, 41–42
—running a losing trade 32–35

making a print 133–134
market(s) 18–19, 58–68; *see
   also* context; information;
   knowledge; price; trading
—activity 13–14, 83
—ahead of participants
   141–142, 147, 148–153
—bear(ish) 54, 61, 67, 78, 94,
   148, 152, 156

—bond 63–65, 78, 79, 84, 86–87, 159
—bull(ish) 12, 40–41, 44, 54, 66, 76, 77, 79, 81, 84, 85, 92, 118, 119, 144, 149, 156, 158
—CDS 64–65, 91, 93
—CFD 21, 62, 68, 100, 101–102, 106, 119, 102
—close 12, 13, 14–15, 87, 88, 109
—commodities 12, 59, 65, 72, 78, 90, 92, 93, 100, 159, 172
—derivatives 66–69, 85, 94, 112, 145, 162, 164, 173, 188, 189
—following several 57–71, 78–80, 81, 85–87, 89–91, 97
—foreign exchange 18, 21, 26–27, 59, 62–63, 73, 78, 81, 84, 87, 100, 101, 102, 106, 119, 144, 159, 164, 166, 187
—futures 10, 11, 16, 59, 62, 63, 65, 66, 68, 74, 84, 87, 90, 92, 94, 100, 101, 102, 103, 105, 106–107, 108, 119, 129, 144, 164, 169, 178, 179, 180, 183
—gold 10, 68, 82, 83, 84, 91, 92, 93, 127–128, 169
—inversely correlated 84–85, 91–92, 179
—knowledge 18–19, 58–68
—opening 12, 13–14, 88–89, 93, 126
—options 13, 66–67, 68, 69, 70, 71, 83, 94, 97, 145, 155, 162, 163–164, 166, 167, 168, 169, 172–173, 184
—participants 11, 12, 18–19, 36, 44, 45–46, 62, 63, 65, 70, 71, 73, 76, 77, 78, 79, 81, 85, 90, 92, 94, 102, 104, 105, 110, 126, 127, 130, 141, 142, 143,

144–146, 148, 150, 152, 157, 168, 172; see also professional traders; traders, retail
—positioning 148, 150, 151, 152, 153, 154, 155, 156, 157–159, 184
—positively correlated 84–85, 91–92, 179
—sentiment and conditions 44, 54, 59, 61, 64, 66, 67, 76, 77, 78, 79, 81, 84, 85, 92, 94, 118, 114, 147, 148, 149, 150, 152, 158
—shares (equities) 5, 11, 12, 14, 18, 40, 44–45, 59–62, 63, 67, 68, 70, 74, 78, 79, 84, 86, 87, 88, 89, 91, 92, 94, 97, 100, 101, 102, 113, 118, 127, 130, 135, 144–145, 149, 156, 158, 163, 164, 165, 166, 172, 173, 178
—trade the 82–84
—understanding 54, 78–79, 85–87
—wrong 145–146
market makers 13, 21, 88–89, 100–102, 118, 143, 166, 176–179, 175–184
media commentators 5, 6, 23, 76, 82, 83
myths of trading 3, 10–22
—no. 1 longer-term trading easier than short-term 10–12
—no. 2 closing prices hold the key 12–15
—no. 3 technical analysis is reliable and successful 15–17
—no. 4 scan through as many contracts as possible to increase your chances of finding a trade 17–19

myths of trading *(cont'd)*
— no. 5 fundamentals, company and economic data are not important 19–20
— no. 6 traders need to buy on the offer side and sell to the bid side of the bid/ask spread 21–22

negative philosophy 46–49
noise 9, 11, 12, 20, 27, 35, 46, 56, 75–7, 87, 98, 109, 130, 177

Open Interest 144, 145
opinions and viewpoints 82–84, 85
options 11, 13, 66–67, 68, 69, 70, 71, 83, 94, 97, 145, 155, 162, 163–164, 166, 167, 168, 169, 172–173, 184
orders 10, 13–14, 21, 28, 62, 102, 126, 178– 179, 182; *see also* stop loss
— limit 13, 179–170
overconfidence 28, 29
overoptimism 29, 59, 78
over-the-counter (OTC) products 13, 102, 112, 164

patterns, seeking 24–26
pension (superannuation) funds 6, 13, 44
platforms 21, 90, 91, 102, 104, 105–107, 110, 111, 113, 114, 179, 183
— market-maker 100–101
position sizing and management 33, 113, 117–138; *see also* pricing in; stop loss orders
— entering a trade 123–127
— managing trades 132–135
— position sizing 119–123

— pricing in 78–79, 140, 154–156, 172
— setting stop loss levels 127–129, 168, 169
— targets 127–129, 133, 138, 169, 172
practising trading 70, 110–11
prediction 25–26, 30, 158
prepared to lose mindset 46–49
price maker 175–184; *see also* market maker
price
— everything is in the 19–20, 78
— closing 12–15, 87–89
— manipulating 88–89
— opening 12, 13, 88
— stock closing
price action 54
pricing in 78–79, 140, 141–159, 172
— examples 148–153
— market reflexivity 156–157
— news 145–146, 148
— outcomes 142–143, 150–151, 158
— position sizing and 154–156
— probability and magnitude 153–155
— vs market is ahead 141–143
probability 24, 25, 26, 42, 49, 51, 125, 152, 153–154, 159, 163, 164, 172
professional traders 9, 10, 12, 14, 45, 46, 48, 55, 58, 67, 83, 93, 104, 122, 125, 126, 123, 143, 169, 175, 176, 183, 186
profit motive 46–49
profits and profitability 6, 8, 13, 16, 21, 22, 32, 36, 40, 42, 44, 45, 47–48, 49, 50–51, 53, 54, 57, 60, 62, 67, 73, 76, 80, 83, 88, 89, 97,

103, 104, 107, 108, 111, 112,
113, 114, 118, 119, 125–126,
130, 131, 136, 139, 142, 146,
147, 155, 157, 158, 175, 177
—bonus 133–134
—flow trading 179, 180, 181,
182, 183, 184,
—giving up 134–135
—run 127, 133, 137
—volatility and 161, 162, 164,
169
proprietary traders 10, 18–19
Prospect Theory 32, 41–42
psychology of traders 23–37; see
also bias; heuristics; weaknesses
of traders

QBE Insurance 149–151, 153, 158

random events 146–147
randomness 17, 24–25, 53
random rewards 25, 49–52, 176,
183
reflexivity in markets 156–157
representativeness bias 24–26
rewards, random 25, 49–52, 176, 183
risk 6, 7, 11, 12, 18, 43, 49, 56, 63
70, 73, 97, 102, 120, 87, 133, 134,
155, 158, 176, 179, 180, 185; see
also behavioural finance; bias;
weaknesses of traders
—assessment 55
—increasing 40, 41, 47, 53, 54,
68, 86–87, 96, 107, 108, 112,
—managing 55, 98, 109, 121,
122, 183
—overnight direction 180, 182,
183–184
—reducing 12, 40–41, 96, 121,
128, 133, 179, 182
—tolerance for 95, 108, 121

risk/reward 11, 18, 49, 66–67, 73,
83, 97, 108, 122, 123, 124, 126,
128, 130, 131, 138, 146,
150–151, 169
rituals 50

salespeople 3–5, 6, 7, 8–9;
see also analysts; brokers; media
commentators; sell side
scalping 101, 107, 108, 179
scratch trades 178, 180
self-attribution bias 26, 29, 35, 45
sell side 4–5, 6, 7, 8–9, 10, 21–22,
34–36, 45, 76, 77, 83
sentiment and conditions, market
44, 54, 59, 61, 64, 66, 67, 76, 77,
78, 79, 81, 84, 85, 92, 94, 118,
114, 147, 148, 149, 150, 152, 158
setting up as a trader 41–43; see also
business, trading as a
settlement of trades 58, 60, 65
shares (equities) 5, 11, 12, 14, 18,
40, 44–45, 60, 61, 62, 63, 67, 68,
74, 78, 79, 84, 86, 87, 88, 89, 91,
92, 94, 97, 100, 101, 102, 113,
118, 127, 130, 135, 144–145,
149, 156, 158, 163, 164, 165,
166, 172, 173, 178; see also short-
selling; stop loss orders
short selling 59–60, 69–71, 158
short cuts 1, 9, 57, 110, 129, 131,
154
—avoiding 54, 137, 138
—desire for 23–37
sideways movement 112, 144, 171
Soros, George 83, 140, 156–157
specialisation, value of 18–19,
73–74, 91, 99–100, 145
status quo bias 32, 35
stock borrow 58, 60–62, 69–70, 78;
see also short selling

stop loss orders 120, 121, 127–132, 137, 168, 168, 169
— activating 131–132
— setting 127–129, 168, 169
— setting small 129–131
— trailing 134–137
strategies, trading 16
support and resistance levels 28, 45, 94, 138
sustainability in trading 1, 6, 20, 23, 40, 43, 54, 56, 57, 58, 71, 84, 97, 109, 114, 125, 130, 154, 162, 175, 177, 185
System 1 (what you see is all there is) 36–37
System 2 36–37, 98, 138
— using 54, 55, 56, 183
systems, trading 31

Taleb, Nassim Nicholas 9, 30, 53, 140
technical analysis 9, 12, 19, 22, 24, 25, 28, 36, 44, 51, 54, 71, 76, 78, 93–94, 107, 124, 125–126, 127, 129, 137, 141, 143, 150–151, 162, 186
— reliability of 15–17, 45–46
Telstra 165–166, 167
tips, ignoring 44
Toshoku 88
trade(s)
— entering a 123–127
— re-entering 33–34, 131
— losing 32–34
— exiting 6, 13, 33, 44
— managing 132–134
— what you see 82–84
traders, professional 175–184
traders, retail see also analysis; biases; business as a trader; heuristics; information; knowledge; market(s); position sizing and

management; price; setting up as a trader; risk; risk/reward; sustainability; trade(s); trading; trading capital; watchlists; weaknesses
— core principles 53–54, 69, 78, 80, 97–98, 117, 138, 162
— goals 40, 54–56, 133
— independent thinking 43–45, 77
— lifestyle 41–43
— Plan B 111–113
— psychology of 23–37
— specialisation, value of 18–19, 73–74, 91, 99–100, 145
— vs sell side 3–7
— weaknesses 23–37
trading see also traders
— all market conditions 40, 53, 54, 66, 67, 69, 112, 113, 138, 147, 162, 168, 183
— benefits of short-term 10–12
— business of 99–115
— capital requirements 107–108
— chart-based 17–18
— contracts 17–19
— flow 178–184
— goals 53–54
— intra-day 10, 169, 179, 184
— practising first 70, 110–11
— reasons for 39–41
— short vs long term 10–11, 74, 140, 157
— time required 108–110
— to win 46–49
— with the trend 15–16
trading account 107, 112, 135
trading capital
— loss of 6, 46–47
— preserving 40, 53, 54, 66, 69, 80, 112, 119, 121, 136, 138, 183
— requirements 107–108

trends 29–30, 49, 155, 168, 170
—trading with 15–16, 43
—trading against 43–44

VIX Index 172–173
volatility 10, 67, 118, 122, 140,
161–174
—appearance of high
170–173
—coping with high
168–169
—defined 162–166
—forecast 163
—future 162
—high 167–173, 182
—historical 162, 163, 164–165,
167–168, 171
—implied 162, 163, 167–168,
173
—using 167–169
Volume-Weighted-Average-Price
(VWAP) orders 13–14

warrants 88–89
watchlists 58, 75–98, 109
—building knowledge through
85–87
—closing price caution 87–89
—constructing 89–93
—context 85–87
—core principles and 97–98
—macro 89–91
—micro 91–93
—overcoming biases with
80–82
—role of 77–78
—trading the markets 82–84, 181
—using to trade 95–96, 145
—watching several markets
78–79, 85–86
weaknesses of traders 23–37, 137;
see also biases
World.com 12

yield curve 64, 77, 79, 85, 91

Learn more with practical advice from our experts

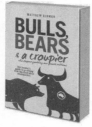

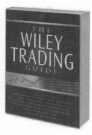
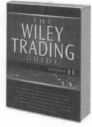